MW01077517

ELEGANT COUNTRY AND SUBURBAN HOUSES OF THE TWENTIES

ELEGANT COUNTRY AND SUBURBAN HOUSES OF THE TWENTIES

Edited by
CHARLES S. KEEFE

DOVER PUBLICATIONS, INC.
Mineola, New York

Bibliographical Note

This Dover edition, first published in 2005, is an unabridged republication of the work originally published by U. P. C. Book Company, Inc., New York, in 1922 under the title *The American House, Being a Collection of Illustrations & Plans of the Best Country & Suburban Houses Built in the United States during the Last Few Years.*

Library of Congress Cataloging in Publication Data

American house.
  Elegant country and suburban houses of the twenties / edited by Charles S. Keefe.
       p. cm.
  Originally published: The American house. New York : U.P.C. Book Co., 1922.
    ISBN 0-486-44216-0 (pbk.)
    1. Architecture, Domestic—United States—20th century. 2. Suburban homes—United States. I. Keefe, Charles S. II. Title.

NA7208.A515 2005
728'.37'0973091733—dc22

                                                                2005043258

Manufactured in the United States of America
Dover Publications, Inc., 31 East 2nd Street, Mineola, N.Y. 11501

FOREWORD

THIS collection of illustrations has been made with the desire to present to the architect and layman, a series of illustrations of the best types of American houses. The illustrations indicate the high standard of our present domestic work and the progress that has been made in recent years. To a person not in close touch with American domestic architecture, it will be a revelation to compare the illustrations in this book with those in architectural books and magazines of fifteen years ago.

Whether our house be large or small, it can be beautiful and a pleasure to ourselves, our friends and to the passerby. While our wants and our pocketbooks determine the size of our house; our own good taste determines its character. This is shown in the illustrations, and houses, such as these, will grow better as age adds its softening touch and they will be good houses as long as they endure.

An attempt has been made to include examples of the various styles suitable for the living conditions in different parts of the country. While the Colonial style seems to predominate, this is explained by the fact that more houses of this style have been erected.

One of the greatest pleasures in owning a fine home is the sharing of its beauties with others, as the owners of these houses have been kind enough to do.

I wish to thank the architects whose work is illustrated; for their aid in securing the material for this book and for the uniform courtesy displayed.

At the same time I wish to express appreciation of the courtesies extended by the editors of The American Architect, Architectural Forum, Architectural Record and Architectural Review.

New York, July, 1921.   Charles S. Keefe.

ERRATA

Plates 21 to 26 inclusive.

The house for Mr. J. M. Townsend, Jr. was designed
by Mr. Bottomley while in the firm of Hewitt & Bottomley, and is now owned by Mr. Faris R. Russell.

Plates 35 to 38 inclusive.

The residence of Col. J. C. Wise should be credited to
Hewitt & Bottomley, as this building was designed by Mr.
Bottomley, while a member of that firm.

LIST OF PLATES

COLONIAL HOUSES

House for J. A. Burden, Esq., Syosset, Long Island.
    Plate No. 1. South Front.
    " " 2. Floor Plans.
    " " 3. Detail of Entrance, North Front.
    " " 4. Loggia.
    " " 5. Entrance, South Front.
    " " 6. Stair Hall and Dining Room.

House of Lathrop Brown, Esq., St. James, Long Island, N. Y.
    Plate No. 7. View from Approach.
    " " 7. View of Central Block.
    " " 8. Floor Plans.
    " " 9. South Elevation.
    " " 10. View across Forecourt.

Country House of Mrs. W. M. Ritter, Manchester, Vt.
    Plate No. 11. Entrance Porch.
    " " 12. Floor Plans.
    " " 13. Entrance Front.
    " " 14. The Stair Hall.

Residence of William Chattin Wetherill, Esq., Laverock, Pa.
    Plate No. 15. Entrance Front.
    " " 16. Floor Plans.
    " " 17. Garden Front.
    " " 18. Living Porch.
    " " 19. Stair Hall.
    " " 20. Den.

House of J. M. Townsend, Jr., Mill Neck, L. I.
    Plate No. 21. Entrance Front.
    " " 22. Floor Plans.
    " " 23. Entrance Doorway.
    " " 24. Entrance, Garden Front.
    " " 25. Living Porch.
    " " 26. Porch and Library.

The Residence of Prof. W. L. Phelps, New Haven, Conn.
    Plate No. 27. Exterior.
    " " 28. Floor Plans.
    " " 29. The Stair Hall.
    " " 30. Dining Room.

Residence of Mrs. William Northrop, Richmond, Va.

Plate No. 31. View of House over Swimming Pool.
" " 32. Floor Plans.
" " 33. Entrance Front.
" " 34. Mantel in Bed Room and Mantel in Dining Room.

Residence of Col. J. C. Wise, Henrico County, Va.

Plate No. 35. Exterior.
" " 36. Floor Plans.
" " 37. Living Room.
" " 38. Living Room Mantel.

Residence of H. F. Atherton, Esq., Brookville, L. I.

Plate No. 39. Entrance Front.
" " 40. Floor Plans.
" " 41. Entrance.

The House of M. A. Lewis, Esq., Hartsdale, N. Y.

Plate No. 42. Doorway.
" " 43. Exterior.
" " 44. Floor Plans.

Residence of Mr. Ellis Y. Brown, Jr., Dowingtown, Pa.

Plate No. 45. View from the Northeast.
" " 46. Floor Plans.
" " 47. East Elevation.
" " 48. Front Door.
" " 49. Dining Room.
" " 50. View of Living Room from Dining Room.

The House of Harvey S. Ladew, Esq., Brookville, L. I.

Plate No. 51. Entrance Front and Garden Front.
" " 52. Floor Plans.
" " 53. The Dining Room.
" " 54. Living Room and a Bed Room.

The House of Miss E. A. Watson, White Plains, N. Y.

Plate No. 55. Entrance Front.
" " 56. Floor Plans.
" " 57. Garden Front.

Farmer's Cottage, Estate of George S. Brewster, Esq., Brookville, Long Island.

Plate No. 58. Exterior and Floor Plans.

House for the Morris Estate, Overbrook, Pa.

Plate No. 59. Entrance Side.
" " 60. Floor Plans.
" " 61. Entrance.
" " 62. Garden Side.

House for Walter C. Baylies, Esq., Taunton, Mass.
 Plate No. 63. Exterior.
 " " 64. Floor Plans.
 " " 65. Entrance Door.
 " " 66. Dining Room.

House of Mr. P. R. Jameson, Esq., Rochester, N. Y.
 Plate No. 67. View from Road.
 " " 68. Floor Plans.

House at Wickford, R. I., for Dr. Harold Metcalf.
 Plate No. 69. Entrance and Floor Plans.
 " " 70. Exterior.

Cottage on Estate of William Chattin Wetherill, Esq., Laverock, Pa.
 Plate No. 71. Entrance Front.
 " " 72. Floor Plans.
 " " 73. View at Rear.
 " " 74. Porch.

House of Mr. Robert Fein, Riverdale, N. Y.
 Plate No. 75. Street Front.
 " " 76. Floor Plans.
 " " 77. Entrance Door.
 " " 78. Detail.

Cottage on Estate of Andrew V. Stout, Esq., Red Bank, N. J.
 Plate No. 79. Exterior and Floor Plans.
 " " 80. Cottage Doorway.

Superintendent's Cottage, Estate of Glenn Stewart, Esq., Locust Valley, L. I.
 Plate No. 81. Exterior and Floor Plans.

Gardener's Cottage for Adolph Mollenhaur., Esq., Bay Shore, L. I.
 Plate No. 82. Exterior and Floor Plans.

GEORGIAN HOUSES

The Country House of Ogden Mills, Esq., Woodbury, L. I.
 Plate No. 83. Entrance Door.
 " " 84. Garden Entrance.
 " " 85. Floor Plans.
 " " 86. Garden Front.
 " " 87. Loggia.

The Country House of Arthur S. Burden, Esq., Jericho, L. I.
 Plate No. 88. Garden Front.
 " " 89. Floor Plan.
 " " 90. Entrance Front.
 " " 91. Entrance.
 " " 92. Garden Steps.
 " " 93. Stair Hall.

Residence of Andrew V. Stout, Esq., Red Bank, N. J.
Plate No. 94.   Entrance Front.
"   "   95.   Floor Plans.
"   "   96.   Entrance Door.
"   "   97.   The Stair Hall.
"   "   98.   Living Room Fire Place.
"   "   99.   Dining Room Fire Place.

Residence of James Swan Frick, Esq., Guilford, Baltimore, Md.
Plate No. 100.   Entrance.
"   "   101.   Floor Plans.
"   "   102.   Garden Front.
"   "   103.   Hallway.
"   "   104.   The Stair Hall.
"   "   105.   The Library.

The Residence of W. F. Hencken, Esq., Greenwich, Conn.
Plate No. 106.   Entrance Court.
"   "   107.   Floor Plans.
"   "   108.   Garden Front.
"   "   109.   Interior Doorway.
"   "   110.   Living Room Fire Place.
"   "   111.   Living Room.

House of Ormsby M. Mitchell, Esq., Rye, N. Y.
Plate No. 112.   View of Forecourt.
"   "   113.   Floor Plans.
"   "   114.   Detail of Sun Room.
"   "   115.   Pool in Garden.
"   "   116.   Living Room.
"   "   117,   Detail of Library Mantel.

The William A. Dixson House, Guilford, Baltimore, Md.
Plate No. 118.   Entrance Front.
"   "   119.   Floor Plans.
"   "   120.   Entrance Door.

Two Semi-Detached Houses for Glenlyon Dye Works, Phillipsdale, R. I.
Plate No. 121.   Exterior and Plan.

House for Mr. James A. Kinghorn, Providence, R. I.
Plate No. 122.   Exterior.
"   "   123.   Entrance and Floor Plan.

Cottage on Estate of Mrs. Charles O. Gates, Locust Valley, Long Island.
Plate No. 124.   Entrance Front.
"   "   125.   Floor Plans.

ITALIAN HOUSES

House of Ernest Allis, Esq., Louisville, Ky.

 Plate No. 126. Entrance.
  " " 127. Entrance Front.
  " " 128. Floor Plans.

House of Harvey Warren, Esq., Forest Hills, L. I.

 Plate No. 129. Front Elevation.
  " " 130. Floor Plans.
  " " 131. Entrance Doorway
  " " 132. Detail of Porch.

Residence of Judge Nash Rockwood, Fieldston, N. Y. C.

 Plate No. 133. Exterior.
  " " 134. Floor Plans.

SPANISH HOUSES

The Major J. H. H. Peshine Residence, Santa Barbara, Cal.

 Plate No. 135. Entrance Front.
  " " 136. Floor Plans.
  " " 137. Chapel with a Glimpse of Patio.
  " " 138. The Patio.

Residence of Tod Ford, Jr., Esq., Pasadena, Cal.

 Plate No. 139. Court and Terrace.
  " " 140. Floor Plans.
  " " 141. Entrance Front.
  " " 142. Exterior.

Residence of T. R. Coffin, Esq., San Marino, Cal.

 Plate No. 143. Entrance Through the Garden.
  " " 144. Floor Plans.

Residence at Santa Barbara, Cal. of George Washington Smith.

 Plate No. 145. Entrance Side.
  " " 146. The Garden Front.
  " " 147. First Floor Plan and Drawing Room.
  " " 148. Second Floor Plan and Drawing Room.

FRENCH HOUSES

Residence of Mr. and Mrs. William Evans, Greenwich, Conn.

 Plate No. 149. Front Elevation.
  " " 150. Floor Plans.
  " " 151. View of Living Room into Hall.
  " " 152. South Porch.
  " " 153. View of Dining Room.
  " " 154. Detail of Dining Room.

A Small House in Los Angeles, California.

 Plate No. 155. Exterior and Floor Plan.

ENGLISH HOUSES

The Residence of Allan S. Lehman, Esq., Tarrytown, N. Y.

    Plate No. 156. Entrance.
      "   " 157. Floor Plans.
      "   " 158. Southeast Elevation.
      "   " 159. Great Hall.
      "   " 160. Southwest View.
      "   " 161. Library.

The House of C. W. Morris, Esq., Haverford, Pa.

    Plate No. 162. South Entrance and Entrance Court.
      "   " 163. Floor Plans.
      "   " 164. The Pool and the Sleeping Porch, and
                     The Pool from the Porch.
      "   " 165. South Facade from Fields and Entrance Hall.
      "   " 166. The Service Court and the Living Room.
      "   " 167. Hallway.

House of Mr. George Arents, Jr., Rye, N. Y.

    Plate No. 168. South Front.
      "   " 169. Floor Plans.
      "   " 170. Entrance.
      "   " 171. South Terrace.
      "   " 172. Garden Pool and Sun Parlor.
      "   " 173. South Elevation from Garden.

Residence for Francis S. McIlhenny, Esq., Chestnut Hill, Pa.

    Plate No. 174. The House from the Highway.
      "   " 175. Floor Plans.
      "   " 176. Main Hall.
      "   " 177. Entrance Loggia.

The House of Joseph and Elizabeth Chamberlain, Middlebury, Conn.

    Plate No. 178. The Entrance.
      "   " 179. Floor Plans.
      "   " 180. View from the Garden.
      "   " 181. View thru Hall.

The House of Jerome Mendleson, Esq., Albany, N. Y.

    Plate No. 182. Exterior.
      "   " 183. Floor Plans.
      "   " 184. Entrance.

Cottage on Estate of Mr. George Arents, Jr., Rye, N. Y.
    Plate No. 185. Front Elevation.

House of Andrew J. Thomas, Esq., Scarsdale, N. Y.

    Plate No. 186. Entrance Front.
      "   " 187. Floor Plans.
      "   " 188. View from Garden.
      "   " 189. The Living Room and the Dining Room.

The Studio Home of Charles E. Chambers, Esq., Riverdale, N. Y.
    Plate No. 190.   Entrance.
    "   " 191.   Floor Plans.
    "   " 192.   Entrance Front.
    "   " 193.   Hall and Dining Room.

INTERIORS

Residence of Mrs. George B. Post, Jr., New York.
    Plate No. 194.   Foyer Hall.

House of Mr. Robert L. Wood, Whitemarsh, Pa.
    Plate No. 195.   Stair Hall.

Harold Carhart Residence, Locust Valley, L. I.
    Plate No. 196.   Hallway.

House of Mr. Fred Dana Marsh, Mural Painter, New Rochelle, N. Y.
    Plate No. 197.   Hallway.

Residence of Mrs. George B. Post, Jr., New York.
    Plate No. 198.   Drawing Room Mantel.

Residence of Mrs. Grenville S. Emmet, New York.
    Plate No. 199.   Library Mantel.

Hugh Legare Residence, Washington, D. C.
    Plate No. 200.   Mantel.

Residence of Albert K. Wampole, Esq., Guilford, Md.
    Plate No. 201.   Mantel in Drawing Room.

W. T. Grant Residence, Pelham, N. Y.
    Plate No. 202.   Living Room.

House of Mrs. William J. Willcox, St. Davids, Pa.
    Plate No. 203.   Living Room.

Harold Carhart Residence, Locust Valley, L. I.
    Plate No. 204.   Dining Room.

House of Mr. Charles M. Hart, Pelham Manor, N. Y.
    Plate No. 205.   Living Room.

House of O. L. Schwenke, Jr.
    Plate No. 206.   Mantel in Hall.

Country House of Jules Breuchaud, Ulster County, N. Y.
    Plate No. 207.   Upper Hall.

House of Mr. Charles M. Hart, Pelham Manor, N. Y.
    Plate No. 208.   Bed Room.

House of Mr. Charles M. Hart, Pelham Manor, N. Y.
    Plate No. 209.   Hallway.

The Dillon House, Kingston, N. Y.
    Plate No. 210.   Hall.

Country House of Jules Breuchaud, Ulster County, N. Y.
    Plate No. 211.   Living Room and Bed Room.

House of Mr. Fred Dana Marsh, Mural Painter, New Rochelle, N. Y.
    Plate No. 212.   Dining Room.

House of Lathrop Brown, Esq., St. James, Long Island, N. Y.
    Plate No. 213.   Living Room in North Wing.

DOORWAYS

Samuel Dwight Brewster Residence, Glen Cove, L. I.
    Plate No. 214.   Doorway.

The House of Dr. T. J. Abbott, Cornwall on Hudson, N. Y.
    Plate No. 215.   Doorway.

William B. Hester Residence, Glen Cove, L. I.
    Plate No. 216.   Doorway.

William Beard Residence, Glen Cove, L. I.
    Plate No. 217.   Entrance Doorway.

J. H. Ottley Residence, Glen Cove, L. I.
    Plate No. 218.   Doorway.

House of Mrs. William J. Willcox, St. Davids, Pa.
    Plate No. 219.   Doorway.

DESCRIPTIVE NOTES

TO simplify the arrangement of the plates, and, it is hoped, to make the book more useful, the buildings have been grouped under their proper styles and a short explanation of each design has been given.

In addition to the complete designs shown, a number of doorways and interiors have been included. It was not possible to show the entire houses in each instance, so the portions that were available have been illustrated when they offered suggestions not covered by the balance of the book.

The descriptions have, purposely, been made simple and concise, because, in the writing of a subject such as the one with which this book deals, it is so easy to wander into generalities that mean nothing.

The term style as applied to the designs in this book must be taken in rather an elastic way. Good designers never slavishly copy a design, but, use in their own way certain forms that determine the style. This gives individuality to a building, that otherwise, it would not have. Also, our buildings are made to fulfill certain wants that did not exist when the various styles were developed. For example; porches and sun rooms must now be incorporated in most plans. All this means a reasonable amount of freedom in following a precedent but does not permit a jumbling of motives from various sources. Therefore it will be understood, that, to a good designer, the word style does not cover a cut and dried formula, to be worked out to the last degree.

COLONIAL HOUSES

PLATES 1-6
HOUSE FOR J. A. BURDEN, ESQ.
SYOSSET, L. I.

The design of this house is refined and has unusual distinction. A pleasing type of Southern Colonial embodying its best traditions both in exterior and plan. The walls are of brick laid in Flemish bond with narrow joints giving a texture in keeping with the design. The cornices, window sills, chimney caps and other details, are of white marble.

It will be noted by referring to the elevations that the house has different floor levels. Two on the garden front, and, three at the entrance front, making a most interesting arrangement.

The plan consists of a central building with flanking wings and pavilions, the principal rooms occupying the central building. On the main floor, the servants' rooms occupy the East wing, while the sons' rooms are situated in the West wing with three guest rooms at the lower level. The principal bed rooms and guest rooms occupy the second floor of the central building.

PLATES 7-10
HOUSE OF LATHROP BROWN, ESQ.
ST. JAMES, LONG ISLAND, N. Y.

This large country house in the Southern Colonial style is one of the best houses in America. While the design was undoubtedly inspired by Westover in Virginia, there has been no attempt to make the new house a copy of the older one. There are two facades; one, facing the water and the other, facing what will later on become a garden. The minor buildings connected to the main building with arched passageways, as at Mount Vernon, give a feeling of spaciousness and breadth to the group.

The color and texture of the walls are uncommon. The bricks slightly larger than usual, are of a pronounced orange pink color, laid in yellow lime with narrow joints.

Petros bleaching lime stone was used for the entrance and other details. With the exception of the entrance doorway and the cornice, everything is very simple and only needs the growth of planting to give it the appearance of settled age.

The plans are ingenious and worthy of thoughtful consideration. A concealed mezzanine floor is carried over the arched passageway at the service wing allowing access to the main house from this part of the group. This arrangement has many advantages, as it does away with the service stairs in the main house, and prevents the kitchen and pantry from being used as a passage way, yet, allowing these rooms to have exposures on two sides.

PLATES 11-14
COUNTRY HOUSE OF MRS. W. M. RITTER
MANCHESTER, VT.

A large New England Colonial house with a plan resembling that of a Southern mansion. It is situated on a hillside at Manchester, Vt. (that town of delightful views) and all of the principal rooms face the view. The exterior is simple with delicate detail and the entrance porch with its bowed front is unusual and charming. The interiors are very interesting and have been furnished with old pieces.

PLATES 15-20
RESIDENCE OF
WILLIAM CHATTIN WETHERILL, ESQ.
LAVEROCK, PA.

It will be observed that Colonial buildings from different sections vary a great deal in character; local conditions and materials being the cause. The style developed in this locality is known as Germantown Colonial and stone was generally used for the walls. While white washing was not often done, the stone work of the Wetherill house has been white washed, as was its prototype "Wyck" at Germantown, but the chimney shows the usual stone work of this section. The plan is long and rambling with the principal rooms opening on a terrace to the South. A view of the hall gives an idea of the charming interior. The room called a

den is really a man's own room, being fitted with work bench, cupboards, etc. It is finished in oak and is a real work shop; something that almost every man would like to possess.

PLATES 21-26
HOUSE OF J. M. TOWNSEND, JR., ESQ.
MILL NECK, L. I.

A straight forward New England Colonial house with a peculiarly well planned interior, for, it is difficult to secure such generous sized rooms with so small an amount of space devoted to the hallways. Doorways open to the North and South and both doorways are original in conception and delightful examples of good taste and refinement in detail. The little library with its panelled walls is just the proper home for good books.

PLATES 27-30
THE RESIDENCE OF PROF. W. L. PHELPS
NEW HAVEN, CONN.

A New England Colonial house that takes its place naturally among its olden time neighbors. Simple and dignified in appearance it follows the best traditions of the old builders.

The walls are of soft red brick and the window sills, lintels and keystones are of white marble. The plan is very convenient and well arranged with the service wing coming at the rear.

The design and furnishings of the interiors are in the same period as the exterior and the result is a most delightful home.

PLATES 31-34
RESIDENCE OF MRS. WILLIAM NORTHROP
RICHMOND, VIRGINIA

This Colonial shingled house with a beautifully detailed entrance porch and doorway has an ideal setting, surrounded as it is by magnificent old trees.

A carefully studied plan gives direct communication between the different parts of the household and all the principal rooms have exposures on two sides. The interiors are carried out with the same delicate detail displayed in the entrance porch.

PLATES 35-38
RESIDENCE OF COL. J. C. WISE
HENRICO COUNTY, VA.

A good example of the type of Colonial houses developed in Virginia. The detail is much bolder than that used for the New England houses of the same period. The visitor to Mount Vernon and other Virginian homes receives this same impression of bold and rather heavy detail, yet, this effect is very charming in the large rooms of these houses. The interiors shown here have all the beauty of the old work in this section.

PLATES 39-41
RESIDENCE OF H. F. ATHERTON, ESQ.
BROOKVILLE, L. I.

The rambling plan and the informal treatment of the exterior of this house gives it all the flavor of an old New England Colonial House. The exterior is simplicity itself. Good window arrangement, different roof levels and the location of the entrance all combine in giving a pleasing result. The curved entrance porch and the doorway have been very well handled.

PLATES 42-44
THE HOUSE OF M. A. LEWIS, ESQ.
HARTSDALE, N. Y.

A Colonial house such as we find on the farms of New England and Eastern New York. It is simple, dignified and homelike, long and rambling with wood shed at the end. The ordinary conception of a Colonial house is one with the windows spaced equidistant from the doorway. This example is less formal as the location of the window openings show.

PLATES 45-50
RESIDENCE OF MR. ELLIS Y. BROWN
DOWNINGTOWN, PA.

To quickly acquire the feeling of having been built for a long time, seems to be one of the attributes of a Germantown Colonial house. The Brown house has this appearance and the pleasing texture of the stone

work is an important part in the result. The broken roof lines, and the porch projecting at a right angle, all tend to suggest a large house when really it is not. The plan is good, all of the principal rooms having two exposures. The porch will look its best when the vines have grown over the lattice work letting in splashes of sunlight here and there. An inviting and delicately detailed doorway forms the entrance to the house. The interiors have been carried out in the same simple style as the exterior and are charming examples of Colonial work.

PLATES 51-54
THE HOUSE OF HARVEY S. LADEW, ESQ.
AT BROOKVILLE, LONG ISLAND

A rambling Long Island Colonial house adapted to present needs. It is a very pleasant and homelike building, with an old fashioned garden and an attractive setting.

This house exhibits the condition that exists where one style is preferred for the exterior and another for the interior. The interiors are English and the Dining Room is particularly good. While the co-ordinating of the two styles has been well done in this instance, it is not a thing to be recommended.

PLATES 55-57
THE HOUSE OF MISS E. A. WATSON
WHITE PLAINS, N. Y.

This is one of the best brick houses in America. When such good effects are produced by such simple means it is not as easy as would appear. Good design and careful detail are responsible for the result.

PLATE 58
FARMER'S COTTAGE
ESTATE OF GEORGE S. BREWSTER, ESQ.
BROOKVILLE, L. I.

This little house follows the precedent set by the Dutch Colonial builders on Long Island. Note the absence of roof overhangs at the gables and the texture of the hand split cypress shingles on the walls.

PLATES 59-62

HOUSE FOR MORRIS ESTATE

OVERBROOK, PA.

A simple Germantown house with all the charm and wholesomeness of this early American style. The entrance with its curved step is charming and the porch with the built-in corners loses the too open appearance that many porches have. The plan is very convenient and the wall with porches at either side effectively conceals the service portion from the garden.

PLATES 63-66

HOUSE FOR WALTER C. BAYLIES, ESQ.

AT TAUNTON, MASS.

A fine example of the rather severe type of New England Colonial. The large central chimney follows the precedent of the houses erected in Connecticut. Narrow clap boards are used for the walls. This house will grow old gracefully.

PLATES 67-68

HOUSE OF P. R. JAMESON, ESQ.

ROCHESTER, N Y.

A very good small Colonial house of brick, sitting well down on the ground. The doorway, with is fan light, is the center of interest in the facade and all the ornament on the exterior is concentrated at the doorway and the main cornice above. The living rooms are located on the garden side of the house, away from the road. A delightful home for a family of moderate size.

PLATES 69-70

HOUSE AT WICKFORD, R. I.

FOR DR. HAROLD METCALF

There is something homelike about the New England Colonial houses. They are simple, straight forward and very inviting. Narrow siding was used for the walls of this house with pilasters at the corners. The doorway is charming.

PLATES 71-74

COTTAGE ON ESTATE OF

WILLIAM CHATTIN WETHERILL, ESQ.

LAVEROCK, PA.

This is a small Germantown Colonial house with whitewashed stonework. The building is low, comfortable and homelike and age will only make it appear better. There is a charm in a building like this that is often lacking in larger buildings.

PLATES 75-78

HOUSE OF MR. ROBERT FEIN

RIVERDALE, N. Y.

A simple Colonial house of brick built on a narrow lot. It exhibits the adaptability of this style to cramped quarters as well as open spaces. It is perfectly possible to design good small houses as this house proves.

PLATES 79-80

COTTAGE ON ESTATE OF

ANDREW V. STOUT, ESQ., RED BANK, N. J.

A little Colonial house with the simplest of plans. The doorway is charming with its seats and the arbor covered with roses. By the way, roses are best to plant at such places as they never completely cover the structure, giving glimpses of it here and there.

PLATE 81

SUPERINTENDENT'S COTTAGE

ESTATE OF GLEN STEWART, ESQ.

LOCUST VALLEY, LONG ISLAND

A true Dutch Colonial type as developed near New York. The long sloping roof, the tall slender columns and the plain wall surface under the porch are all suggestive of this charming style. The absence of dormers is quite usual in these houses.

PLATE 82

GARDENER'S COTTAGE

FOR ADOLPH MOLLENHAUER, ESQ.

BAY SHORE, LONG ISLAND

A little Colonial farm house of the simplest type. The porch forms the center of interest in the main facade and the walls are covered with hand split cypress shingles with ends squared.

GEORGIAN HOUSES

PLATES 83-87

THE COUNTRY HOUSE OF

OGDEN MILLS, ESQ.

WOODBURY, L. I.

A large country house, following Georgian traditions, that have been handled in an original way; both in plans and exterior.

The main mass of the house occupys the center of the composition, with wings at either side forming courts. Only the main house is two stories high, all of the wings being one story in height, and one room in width. Planning in this way gives great openness and breadth to the building and there is no massing of rooms in the center as frequently occurs where a large number of rooms are planned for.

The exterior is of dark red brick with lime stone for the doorways, cornices and columns. The details suggest the work of the Adam brothers, especially the columns and the circular panels in the walls. It is a fine, distinguished mansion of great beauty and will grow better with time. The interiors were not available for publication.

PLATES 88-93

THE COUNTRY HOUSE OF

ARTHUR S. BURDEN, ESQ., JERICHO, L. I.

An original and distinguished piece of work well handled. This beautifully proportioned Georgian house has the appearance of having existed in its environment for many years.

The wings have been kept at a lower level emphasizing the importance of the main building and the flat pilasters on the walls add to this effect. The house is in such intimate touch with the surrounding gardens and lawns that it is only a step through the casement doors to the ground.

The interiors are stately and formal and the graceful stairway winding its way upward is a delightful piece of design. At the terrace the curved steps and iron railing add grace to an altogether pleasing garden.

PLATES 94-99

RESIDENCE OF ANDREW V. STOUT, ESQ.

RED BANK, N. J.

A simple well proportioned Georgian house. The mass is good and the spacing of the window openings has been well handled. The brick walls have a lovely texture and the sills and other details are of marble rather two white in contrast with the walls, but time will remedy this.

The house is symetrical in plan and all of the principal rooms have two exposures.

A designer has to be very sure of himself to attempt a stairway such as this house possesses. It is unusually successful and very graceful. The interiors are bits of good design delicately detailed. Over the dining room mantel is a panel containing a map of the surrounding country together with a dial indicating the direction of the prevailing wind. The dial is connected with a vane on the roof and works automatically.

PLATES 100-105

RESIDENCE OF JAMES SWAN FRICK

GUILFORD, BALTIMORE, MD.

One of the best of our Georgian houses. The walls are of brick laid in Flemish bond with white mortar and the cornices and other details are of Indiana limestone.

The architect has been very skillful in designing such a compact and well arranged plan which provides for rooms of fine scale and proportion. The interiors are lofty and spacious and very beautiful in design and furnishings. The style is that of the Adam brothers at their best. In the library the wood work is American walnut which forms a fine setting for the brighter colored books.

PLATES 106-111

THE RESIDENCE OF W. F. HENCKEN, ESQ.

GREENWICH, CONN.

An informal Georgian house of brick, with rough stone sills almost the same color as the brick. The house has been kept quite low and the effect is simple and good. The texture of the wall is interesting, a rather rough, hard burned brick, being used. Limestone being employed for the doorway and cornices. Casement sashes were used for the windows; giving the house the appearance of one of the simpler English Georgian houses. The interiors are extremely livable and are fine examples of good design and furnishing. The designer was able to secure these pleasing and delightful results by the simplest of means as the living room shows. Delicately detailed cornices add much to the rooms.

PLATES 112-117
HOUSE OF ORMSBY M. MITCHELL, ESQ.
RYE, N. Y.

A Georgian house of moderate size and of good design. While this style is adapted to both town and country conditions, it appears to best advantage as the illustrations show when set in spacious well kept grounds. The living porch has been well handled. We Americans have developed the porch, until it is now an outdoor room, used more or less all the year. To keep it open enough to be comfortable in summer and still enclosed enough to appear as a room, is not the most simple of problems.

The interiors are distinguished examples of good design and furnishing, following the same precedent as the exterior.

PLATES 118-120
THE WILLIAM A. DIXSON HOUSE
AT GUILFORD, BALTIMORE, MD.

A small house designed in the Georgian manner. The property is rather restricted in size yet there is no suggestion of this in the plan or exterior. The principal rooms are situated on the garden side of the house, most of the rooms having this exposure. The street front of the house proper is symetrical with well disposed openings. An old panel has been placed in the pediment of the finely proportioned doorway. This panel is one of those placed on the early houses of Philadelphia, marking them as having been in-

sured against fire and securing for them all help possible in times of danger.

The building has been carefully planned and the little court yard at the garage is very well arranged. A very pleasant and comfortable home.

PLATE 121
TWO SEMI-DETACHED HOUSES
FOR THE GLENLYON DYE WORKS
PROVIDENCE, R. I.

These houses are interesting because of the simple way in which the problem was solved. The design somewhat influenced by Georgian work is straight forward and the lines are good. An every day problem much better done than ordinarily. The neglect of good design in houses of this sort is the thing that makes the streets of many American towns such dreary affairs. We are understanding more and more the effect of a man's environment upon his character and the best way to start social improvement is in the houses of the workers.

PLATES 122-123
HOUSE FOR MR. JAMES A. KINGHORN
PROVIDENCE, R. I.

A small Georgian house with its end to the street. The entrance is at the side allowing the main rooms to secure the best exposures, a slightly bowed bay at the entrance effectively breaks what would have otherwise been a plain straight wall.

PLATES 124-125
COTTAGE ON ESTATE OF
MRS. CHARLES O. GATES,
LOCUST VALLEY, L. I.

A picturesque little brick house with Georgian influence in its design. It is quaint, very small and homelike and is an answer to those who do not believe that little houses deserve more attention than they have been receiving.

ITALIAN HOUSES

PLATES 126-128
HOUSE OF ERNEST ALLIS ESQ.
LOUISVILLE, KENTUCKY

A dignified example of an American house in the Italian style. The entrance doorway is particularly worthy of notice, both for its design and setting. The plan is arranged so that the main portion of the house is but one room in depth. This affords cross ventilation, a most desirable feature where the summers are warm. When results can be as successful as this it seems a pity that more houses of this style are not erected.

PLATES 129-132
HOUSE OF HARVEY WARREN, ESQ.
FOREST HILLS, LONG ISLAND

A house of moderate size and following Italian precedents. The stucco has been roughened giving it the appearance of Travertine and the roof tiles have been roughly cemented to give more texture to the surface. The plans have been carefully worked out for the needs of a family living in a suburban community and are very convenient. Distinctive in design and well placed, is the porch opening from the living room.

PLATES 133-134
RESIDENCE OF JUDGE NASH ROCKWOOD
FIELDSTON, N. Y. C.

An American adaption of the Italian style. The material is stucco with a sand floated finish. The design is good and shows how adaptable this style is for our houses. The sills and quoins and other projections give the best results when kept rather flat as they have been in this case.

SPANISH HOUSES

PLATES 135-138
THE MAJOR J. H. H. PESHINE RESIDENCE
SANTA BARBARA, CALIFORNIA

This house was erected for a decendant of a noble Spanish family which obtained a large grant of land at Santa Barbara from the King of Spain. The house was built among the old olive trees and against the hillside which slopes up sharply at the rear of the patio. It is eminently fitted to its environment and is a fine example of the Spanish style.

PLATES 139-142
RESIDENCE OF TOD FORD, ESQ.
PASADENA, CALIFORNIA

There is a logical type of building fitted for each locality and the Spanish and Italian styles seem to belong to the soil and climate of California, as well as they do to their native habitats. The beautiful effects achieved with such simple means in this rather rambling house are worthy of careful study. The use of great wall spaces with roofs at different levels and the careful placing of the window openings are all responsible for the results. The planting with the light stucco walls for a background is unusually successful.

PLATES 143-144
RESIDENCE OF T. R. COFFIN, ESQ.
SAN MARINO, CALIFORNIA

Buildings like the Coffin house seem to belong to their environment. These little Spanish buildings need brilliant sunshine and a climate like California's to appear at their best. The brilliant stucco of the walls and the soft hues of the hand made tiles are lovely when used in such a place. There is no patio, the windows of the principal room opening onto the terrace and the lawn. The plan is good, and, rambling enough to make it picturesque.

PLATES 145-148

RESIDENCE AT SANTA BARBARA, CALIFORNIA

FOR GEORGE WASHINGTON SMITH

The idea for this interesting house was taken from a thirteenth century Spanish house and the decoration is so simple that it might belong to any period. The roof tiles are hand made, then baked, but not glazed. They are a soft red in color and form a fine contrast to the brilliant stucco of the walls. The window frames and sashes are painted a rich Gothic blue.

The plan is as simple and direct as the exterior and the interiors have all the flavor of old world rooms. The walls are treated in softly modelled plaster and form a fine back ground for the furniture. The brilliant colors of the upholstery and hangings give a restful and livable look to the rooms and the effect is beautiful.

FRENCH HOUSES

PLATES 149-154

RESIDENCE OF

MR. AND MRS. WILLIAM EVANS

GREENWICH, CONN.

Our ways of living are so different from the French that this style is rarely used in America. Few architects are capable of approaching the subject in such a sympathetic way as the architects of this building have done. While it follows rather closely the lines of the Petit Trianon at Versailles this house has an individuality of its own. It is very formal and stately, yet, lovely. The plans are ingenious; advantage being taken of the symetrical plan to make this a very livable house. The interiors are lofty, airy and dignified and altogether beautiful. The style is late Louis XV and early Louis XVI.

PLATE 155

A SMALL HOUSE IN LOS ANGELES

CALIFORNIA

The design of this house was inspired by the farm cottages of France where the architect served during the war. A house of this kind is adaptable to other parts of the country, which is true of very few Californian houses. This little house is quaint and homelike and nestles down contentedly in its rather barren environment.

ENGLISH HOUSES

PLATES 156-161

THE RESIDENCE OF

ALLAN S. LEHMAN, ESQ.

TARRYTOWN, N. Y.

A very picturesque English Tudor house in a wonderfully fine setting. Rough old bricks, red in color, were used for the walls and lime stone was used at the windows and doorways. The half timber has a weathered finish and the verge boards at the gables are carved.

The roof slates are graduated in thickness and exposure to the weather giving most interesting roof surfaces. The plan, it will be observed is very simple and direct. Following the precedent of the Tudor mansion, the Great Hall is the center about which the minor rooms are grouped and remains the center of the domestic life of the household.

This hall is of magnificent proportions as is also the Great Hall window which faces the West. The library is a delightful room with its oak paneling and ornamental plaster ceiling, and the house as a whole is a charming example of consistency in design and furnishing.

PLATES 162-167

THE HOUSE OF C. W. MORRIS, ESQ.

HAVERFORD, PA.

An interesting combination in brick, stucco and half timber with many breaks in the plan and irregular roofs. The wood beams, used for posts and lintels and half timber work, have been adzed, and wooden pegs are used in the half timber work, in a decorative way. Warmth and color are given by the use of brick at the window and door jambs and at the chimneys. The casement sash are of metal with leaded lights making the most pleasant of windows.

Every turn around the house brings another surprise and another delightful view. The designer evidently had as much pleasure, in working out the design, as he gives the observer. It is all very English and suggestive of pleasant ways of living.

The plan of this house is so arranged that all the principal rooms face the South. The living porch is located on the Southwest corner and opens on three sides to catch every breeze. All the principal rooms of the house are in close touch with the gardens and overlook the best views.

The service portion is placed where it does not interfere with the views, yet is convenient, and forms one side of the Fore court, making a most effective entrance.

Most of the interiors are treated with wood beamed ceilings and plastered walls hand finished in an antique way. Wood work has been eliminated around the interior openings and the floor boards are of irregular widths.

PLATES 168-173
HOUSE OF MR. GEORGE ARENTS, JR.
RYE, N. Y.

The English ways of living are much like our own, and, since we have taken more and more to country life it is natural that we should adopt the Elizabethan style for some of our houses. This is especially so in the East where sections of the country are very much like the English countryside.

The Arents' house while quite large settles well down on the ground and the land slopes gently away from it on all sides. At one end a garden, enclosed by a wall, has been carried out on a level. The sun porch opens on this enclosed garden with a pool directly in front of it, reflecting the house and surroundings in its surface. The house is irregular in form with terraces at different levels making a most charming setting.

The house walls are of brick laid with rather close joints and the trim is of Indiana limestone. Patterns have been introduced

in the brick work at the gables of the garden facade giving a most pleasing effect. This house is distinguished by its design and beautiful detail.

PLATES 174-177
RESIDENCE OF
FRANCIS S. MCILHENNY, ESQ.
CHESTNUT HILL, PA.

In European countries the service buildings are often connected to the main building and form an interesting part of the group. This has not appealed to the American taste, as we prefer to have the odors and flies removed as far as possible from our living quarters. Since the motor has replaced the horse, these objections are removed, in part, and, the garage and other unobjectionable service buildings are often incorporated in the house group. In the McIlhenny house the service buildings form one side of the fore court and screen the service court. The layout has been so carefully planned that the main house is in intimate touch with the grounds on the three sides. On the east the paved terrace and the living porch open onto the garden with the swimming pool at the other end. At both sides of this enclosed garden are walks leading to the pool. The exterior is modern English with stone walls pointed flush giving them a pleasing texture. A view of the entrance across the fore court is charming as the illustration shows and the loggia opening on the sunken garden has all the flavor of an old world building.

The interiors have been carried out in hand finished plaster, while the important rooms have wood beamed ceilings and tile floors.

PLATES 178-181
THE HOUSE OF
JOSEPH AND ELIZABETH CHAMBERLAIN
MIDDLEBURY, CONN.

The English have a way of making the garden an intimate part of the menage. The garden becomes a part of the house, as it were, and is used as such. In the Chamberlain house this has been accomplished by the simplest of means. The summer house or rather the outdoor room overlooking the sunken garden is tied to the house by the garden wall making it an important part of the composition.

The entrance is delightfully informal with the paved space before it and the chairs awaiting the visitor. The long sloping roof comes well down over the entrance giving a low comfortable appearance to the house, and quaint dormers breaking the roof surface at intervals add interest to the effect. The whole plan reflects sensible living and the love of home and the out of doors.

PLATES 182-184
THE HOUSE OF JEROME MENDLESON, ESQ.
ALBANY, NEW YORK

A brick house has a charm all its own and when the style is English, it seems to impress this charm more forcibly upon us. In the Mendleson house, rather steep pitched roofs sloping down at either end give a breadth to the design, that would otherwise be lacking. Dark brick with rather narrow joints have been used for the walls and the variegated slate on the roof are graduated giving a very pleasing texture to this surface. A doorway of white marble is the center of the composition and adds the only touch of ornament to the facade. The doorway is most graceful and emphasizes the hospitality that waits beyond.

All the principal rooms on the first floor open upon a terrace at the garden side of the house. The service wing is ingeniously concealed behind the mass of the house, without interfering with the view to the garden from the main rooms.

PLATE 185
COTTAGE ON
ESTATE OF MR. GEORGE ARENTS, JR.
RYE, NEW YORK

Large wall surfaces look well when properly handled and can be made decidedly interesting. The concentration of the windows at a few points in this Modern English house gives this result. The graduated slate roof is well worth attention and emulation.

PLATES 186-189
HOUSE OF ANDREW J. THOMAS, ESQ.
SCARSDALE, NEW YORK

An example of modern English work, with very few window openings, which is characteristic of these houses. Rough cast stucco was used for the walls and graduated slate for the roof. The plan is good and very convenient.

With such simple interiors the effects depend altogether upon the furniture which must consist of a few, but good pieces, carefully disposed. The solid color rug in the dining room, takes its place more naturally with this simple style than do the Oriental rugs in the living room.

PLATES 190-193
THE STUDIO HOME OF
CHARLES E. CHAMBERS, ESQ.
RIVERDALE, N. Y.

It is rather difficult to place this house exactly, tho one might call it English, influenced by early German work. It has interesting lines and the materials employed are stone and stucco. The interiors are distinguished by the good taste shown in the furnishings.

INTERIORS.

In glancing thru the interiors shown here, as well as in the other portion of the book, it will be observed that there is a great deal of variety in the designs. They range from formal country mansions, to those of simple farm house interiors; some are intended for high heeled slippers and silken gowns, and in others we can see, in our mind's eye, a group, clad in tweeds gathered about the hospitable fire place, after a day in the open. It is all a part of our lives and these interiors are alike in one respect, in that they are all good.

Observe the means and materials used in securing the desired effects. If any lesson can be learned from the study of these interiors, it is that good decoration is as varied as our needs and purses.

PLATE 194
HOUSE OF MRS. GEORGE B. POST, JR.
FOYER HALL

A delightful bit of design, is this hall, in the Italian manner. It is quiet and restful with no elaborate detail or straining after an effect. The reveals at the archway and panel are most delicate in their refinement.

PLATE 195
STAIR HALL OF ROBERT L. WOOD

A Colonial hallway of good design and proportion effectively furnished. The carpet rug of solid color is just right. If the rather large radiator could have been concealed the result would have been perfect.

PLATE 196
HALLWAY, HAROLD CARHART RESIDENCE.

The broad spacious hall of a country house. The walls and ceiling are painted in the same color as the wood work, and the stair railing is of mahogany. Ornamental panels alternate—with plain balusters at the stairs—in the manner of the old Salem stairways. A most pleasing and gracious entrance to a home.

PLATES 197 AND 212
INTERIORS, HOUSE OF
FRED DANA MARSH, MURAL PAINTER

Two rooms that can be credited to no particular style. They are pleasant and satisfying and very original in their treatment. In the hall the white walls of panelled wood emphasize the beauty of the hangings. The decoration on the door in the Dining Room was painted by the owner. The walls of this room are white with decorations in black.

PLATE 198
RESIDENCE OF MRS. GEORGE B. POST, JR.
DRAWING ROOM MANTEL

A room in the Italian manner with a small mantel in stone and an old portrait well hung. It is all admirably composed and effective.

PLATE 199
RESIDENCE OF MRS. GRENVILLE S. EMMET
LIBRARY MANTEL

A very simple Georgian mantel of marble, happily placed. The right mantel, a few good furnishings well disposed and the composition is complete.

PLATE 200
MANTEL, HUGH LEGARE RESIDENCE

A mantel in a panelled room, with carving after the manner of Grinling Gibbons. The simple stone architrave around the fire place opening, acts as a foil to the elaborate carving above. A good piece of design, with all the pleasing qualities of an old room.

PLATE 201
HOUSE OF ALBERT K. WAMPOLE
MANTEL IN DRAWING ROOM

Mantel of colored marbles most effectively placed in the side of a panelled room. It is all reminiscent of the best Georgian work and a period of English life co-existent with our best Southern Colonial.

PLATE 202
W. T. GRANT RESIDENCE
LIVING ROOM

A room that is Italian in feeling and furnishing yet containing a number of pieces of furniture from other periods. The result is very satisfying. Good pieces of furniture from various periods may be used without causing disturbance when done as well as in this room.

PLATE 203
LIVING ROOM OF MRS. WILLIAM J. WILCOX

An English room with sand finished plaster walls and oak paneling across the fire place end. The generous fire place and this simple style reflect an informal period of English work and very pleasant ways of living.

PLATE 204
HAROLD CARHART RESIDENCE
DINING ROOM,

This room with walls paneled in painted pine, follows the precedent of the old Colonial country houses near Philadelphia.

Formal and stately it brings to mind the period of Washington and Ben Franklin when our country was in the making.

PLATES 205-208 AND 209
HOUSE OF MR. CHARLES M. HART
INTERIORS

The interiors of this house form an admirable back ground for the pieces of early American furniture with which it is furnished. The living room with its simple mantel with cupboards above and the hallway with the curved railing at the stairway are in just the right spirit. The bed room with the ceiling cut off at the corners is a delightful room. It is just such a room as we read about in the old story books. The window hangings are worthy of note.

PLATE 206
HOUSE OF O. L. SCHWENKE, JR.
MANTEL IN HALL

A little bit of the early part of the last century. The mantel, wall paper and furnishings are just right making a lovely little room.

PLATES 207 AND 211
COUNTRY HOUSE OF JULES BREUCHAUD
INTERIORS

The interiors of the Breuchaud house are admirable examples of the old Dutch work in Ulster County, N. Y. Both the architect and the owner must have a very sympathetic understanding of this style to secure such pleasing results. There is an atmosphere of rest and quiet about the rooms.

PLATE 210
HALL, THE DILLON HOUSE
KINGSTON, N. Y.

A quaint little hallway with a fine old mantel; Dutch tiles with blue figures are used for the facings at the fire place. The beams overhead are exposed and the ceiling is formed by the floor boards above. All in the spirit of the old Dutch builders at Kingston, New York.

PLATE 213
HOUSE OF LATHROP BROWN, ESQ.
LIVING ROOM IN NORTH WING

A room finished with painted early eighteenth century Georgian panels. This room will later on become the schoolroom, being temporarily used as a living room until the main rooms are completed. Refer to plates seven and ten for illustrations of this house.

DOORWAYS.

There is something particularly inviting and pleasing about Colonial and Georgian doorways. In many of the early houses it was only at the entrance door and porch, that the architect or builder "let go" as it were and gave us an idea of how much knowledge he really possessed.

These early designers devoted a great deal of thought and attention to this feature of the design and in our Colonial houses it is a poor house that does not boast of at least one good doorway. Even the most simple examples exhibit signs of having been carefully studied and proportioned.

The architects of today are following in the footsteps of the old builders and the illustrations show that good taste and careful study are amply repaid when intelligently applied.

Plate 214.

A stately well proportioned Colonial doorway for a large country house.

Plate 215.

One of the most charming of our modern examples of Georgian doorways.

Plate 216.

A formal Colonial entrance for a country house. The planting when grown will add much to the design.

Plate 217.

A little Colonial doorway with a pediment and a fan light of leaded glass. Quaint and interesting with very good planting.

Plate 218.

A Colonial doorway with fan light and side lights. A very interesting design with beautiful detail, somewhat influenced by the Greek revival.

Plate 219.

A very simple and pleasing Germantown doorway. The little trellis over the door adds much to the effect.

COLONIAL HOUSES

SOUTH FRONT

HOUSE FOR J. A. BURDEN, ESQ., SYOSSET, L. I.

DELANO AND ALDRICH, ARCHITECTS

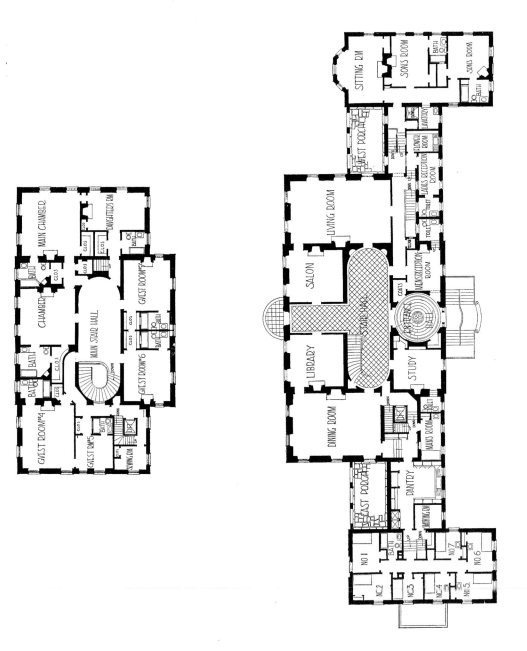

FLOOR PLANS

HOUSE FOR J. A. BURDEN, ESQ., AT SYOSSET, L. I.

DELANO AND ALDRICH, ARCHITECTS

DETAIL OF ENTRANCE, NORTH FRONT

HOUSE FOR J. A. BURDEN, ESQ., SYOSSET, L. I.

DELANO AND ALDRICH, ARCHITECTS

LOGGIA

HOUSE FOR J. A. BURDEN, ESQ., SYOSSET, L. I.

DELANO AND ALDRICH, ARCHITECTS

ENTRANCE SOUTH FRONT

HOUSE FOR J. A. BURDEN, ESQ., SYOSSET, L. I.

DELANO AND ALDRICH, ARCHITECTS

STAIR HALL

DINING ROOM

HOUSE FOR J. A. BURDEN, ESQ., AT SYOSSET, L. I.

DELANO AND ALDRICH, ARCHITECTS

VIEW FROM APPROACH

VIEW OF CENTRAL BLOCK

HOUSE OF LATHROP BROWN, ESQ., ST. JAMES, LONG ISLAND, N. Y.

PEABODY, WILSON AND BROWN, ARCHITECTS

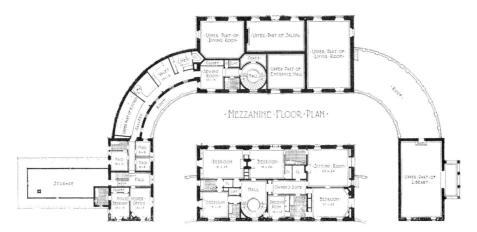

·MEZZANINE·FLOOR·PLAN·

·SECOND·FLOOR·PLAN·

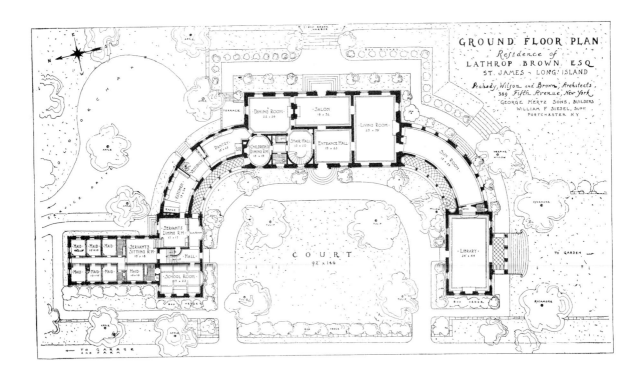

GROUND FLOOR PLAN
Residence of
LATHROP BROWN, ESQ
ST. JAMES — LONG ISLAND

Peabody, Wilson and Brown, Architects
389 Fifth Avenue, New York
GEORGE MERTZ SONS, BUILDERS
WILLIAM F. SIESEL, SUPT
PORTCHESTER, N.Y.

FLOOR PLANS

HOUSE OF LATHROP BROWN, ESQ., ST. JAMES, LONG ISLAND, N. Y.

PEABODY, WILSON AND BROWN, ARCHITECTS

SOUTH ELEVATION

HOUSE OF LATHROP BROWN, ESQ., ST. JAMES, LONG ISLAND, N. Y.

PEABODY, WILSON AND BROWN, ARCHITECTS

VIEW ACROSS FORECOURT

HOUSE OF LATHROP BROWN, ESQ., ST. JAMES, LONG ISLAND, N. Y.

PEABODY, WILSON AND BROWN, ARCHITECTS

ENTRANCE PORCH

COUNTRY HOUSE OF MRS. W. M. RITTER, MANCHESTER, VT.

MURPHY AND DANA, ARCHITECTS

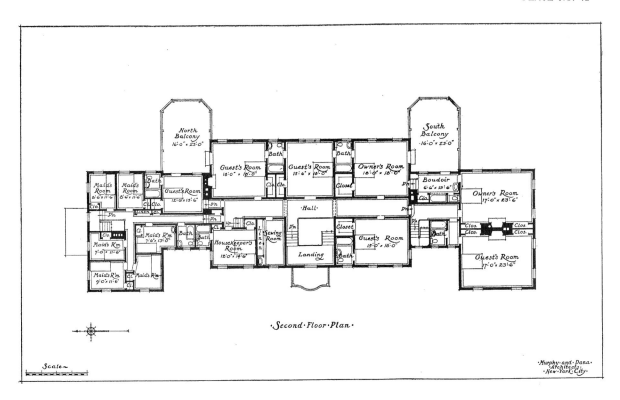

·Second·Floor·Plan·

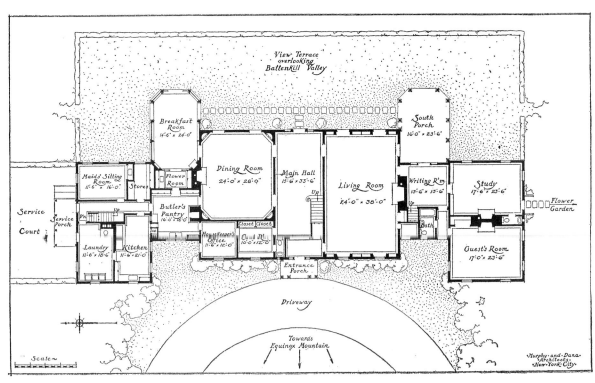

FLOOR PLANS

COUNTRY HOUSE OF MRS. W. M. RITTER, MANCHESTER, VT.

MURPHY AND DANA, ARCHITECTS

ENTRANCE FRONT

COUNTRY HOUSE OF MRS. W. M. RITTER, MANCHESTER, VT.

MURPHY AND DANA, ARCHITECTS

THE STAIR HALL

COUNTRY HOUSE OF MRS. W. M. RITTER, MANCHESTER, VT.

MURPHY AND DANA, ARCHITECTS

ENTRANCE FRONT

RESIDENCE OF WM. CHATTIN WETHERILL, ESQ., LAVEROCK, PA.

JOHN GRAHAM, JR., ARCHITECT

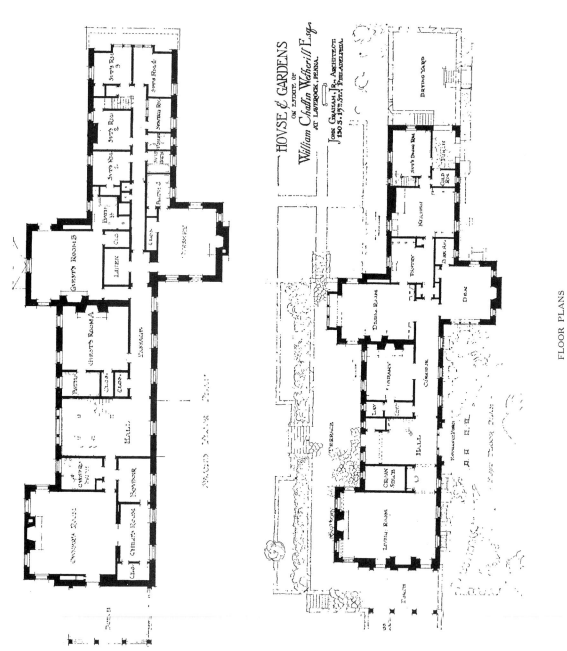

FLOOR PLANS

RESIDENCE OF WM. CHATTIN WETHERILL, ESQ., LAVEROCK, PA.

JOHN GRAHAM, JR., ARCHITECT

GARDEN FRONT

RESIDENCE OF WM. CHATTIN WETHERILL, ESQ., LAVEROCK, PA.

JOHN GRAHAM, JR., ARCHITECT

LIVING PORCH

RESIDENCE OF WM. CHATTIN WETHERILL, ESQ., LAVEROCK, PA.

JOHN GRAHAM, JR., ARCHITECT

STAIR HALL

RESIDENCE OF WM. CHATTIN WETHERILL, ESQ., LAVEROCK, PA.

JOHN GRAHAM, JR., ARCHITECT

DEN

RESIDENCE OF WM. CHATTIN WETHERILL, ESQ., LAVEROCK, PA.

JOHN GRAHAM, JR., ARCHITECT

ENTRANCE GARDEN FRONT

HOUSE OF J. M. TOWNSEND, JR., MILL NECK, L. I.

WM. LAWRENCE BOTTOMLEY, ARCHITECT

FLOOR PLANS

HOUSE OF J. M. TOWNSEND, JR., MILL NECK, L. I.

WM. LAWRENCE BOTTOMLEY, ARCHITECT

ENTRANCE DOORWAY
HOUSE OF J. M. TOWNSEND, JR., MILL NECK, L. I.
WM. LAWRENCE BOTTOMLEY, ARCHITECT

ENTRANCE FRONT

HOUSE OF J. M. TOWNSEND, JR., MILL NECK, L. I.

WM. LAWRENCE BOTTOMLEY, ARCHITECT

LIVING PORCH

HOUSE OF J. M. TOWNSEND, JR., MILL NECK, L. I.

WM. LAWRENCE BOTTOMLEY, ARCHITECT

PORCH

LIBRARY

HOUSE OF J. M. TOWNSEND, JR., MILL NECK, L. I.

WM. LAWRENCE BOTTOMLEY, ARCHITECT

EXTERIOR

THE RESIDENCE OF PROF. W. L. PHELPS, NEW HAVEN, CONN.

MURPHY AND DANA, ARCHITECTS

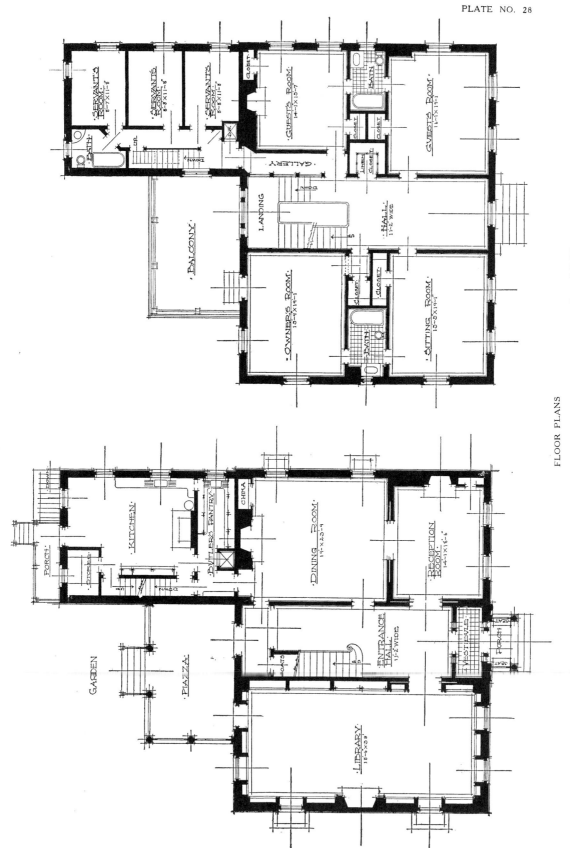

FLOOR PLANS

THE RESIDENCE OF PROF. W. L. PHELPS, NEW HAVEN, CONN.

MURPHY AND DANA, ARCHITECTS

THE STAIR HALL

THE RESIDENCE OF PROF. W. L. PHELPS, NEW HAVEN, CONN.

MURPHY AND DANA, ARCHITECTS

DINING ROOM

THE RESIDENCE OF PROF. W. L. PHELPS, NEW HAVEN, CONN.

MURPHY AND DANA, ARCHITECTS

VIEW OF HOUSE OVER SWIMMING POOL

RESIDENCE OF MRS. WILLIAM NORTHROP, RICHMOND, VA.

WALTER D. BLAIR, ARCHITECT

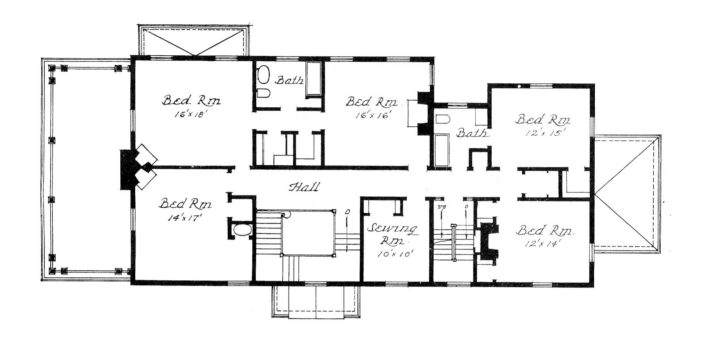

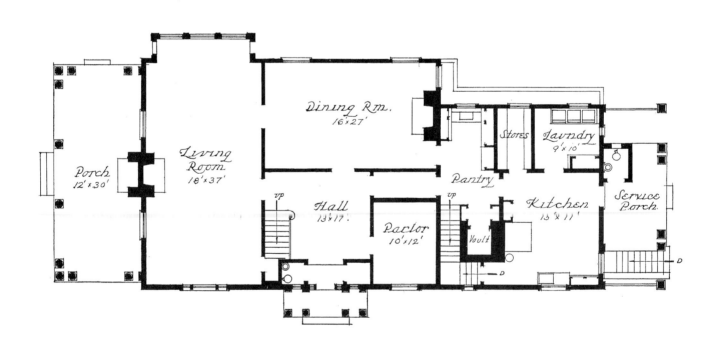

FLOOR PLANS

RESIDENCE OF MRS. WILLIAM NORTHROP, RICHMOND, VA.

WALTER D. BLAIR, ARCHITECT

ENTRANCE PORCH
RESIDENCE OF MRS. WILLIAM NORTHROP, RICHMOND, VA,
WALTER D. BLAIR, ARCHITECT

MANTEL IN DINING ROOM

MANTEL IN BED ROOM

RESIDENCE OF MRS. WILLIAM NORTHROP, RICHMOND, VA.

WALTER D. BLAIR, ARCHITECT

EXTERIOR

RESIDENCE OF COL. J. C. WISE, HENRICO COUNTY, VA.

WM. LAWRENCE BOTTOMLEY, ARCHITECT

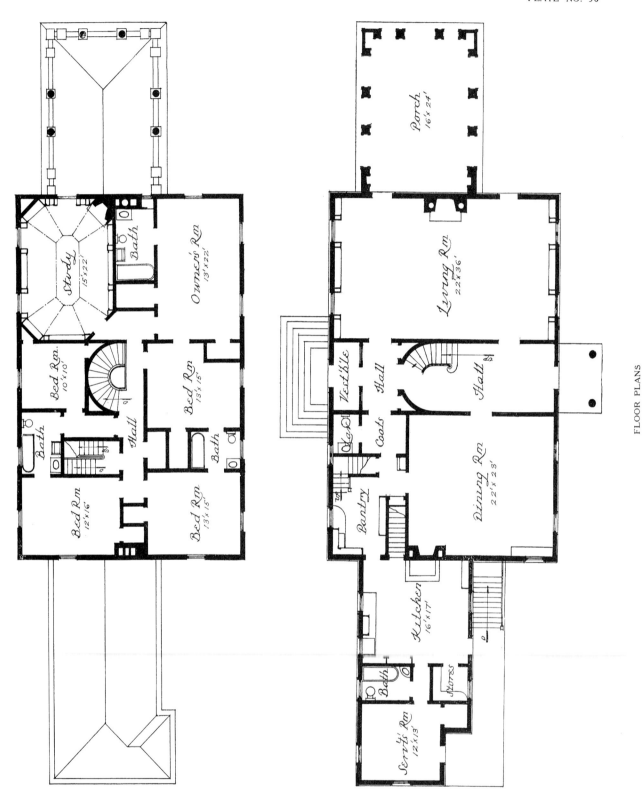

Study
15' x 22'

Bath

Owner's Rm
13' x 22'

Bed Rm.
10' x 10'

Bath

Hall

Bed Rm
13' x 15'

Bed Rm
12' x 16'

Bath

Bed Rm
13' x 15'

Porch
16' x 24'

Living Rm
22' x 36'

Vest'b'le

Hall

Coats

Hall

Pantry

Dining Rm
22' x 23'

Kitchen
16' x 17'

Bath

Stores

Serv'ts' Rm
12' x 13'

FLOOR PLANS

RESIDENCE OF COL. J. C. WISE, HENRICO COUNTY, VA.

WM. LAWRENCE BOTTOMLEY, ARCHITECT

LIVING ROOM

RESIDENCE OF COL. J. C. WISE, HENRICO COUNTY, VA.

WM. LAWRENCE BOTTOMLEY, ARCHITECT

LIVING ROOM MANTEL
RESIDENCE OF COL. J. C. WISE, HENRICO COUNTY, VA.
WM. LAWRENCE BOTTOMLEY, ARCHITECT

ENTRANCE FRONT

RESIDENCE OF H. F. ATHERTON, ESQ., BROOKVILLE, L. I.

JAMES W. O'CONNOR, ARCHITECT

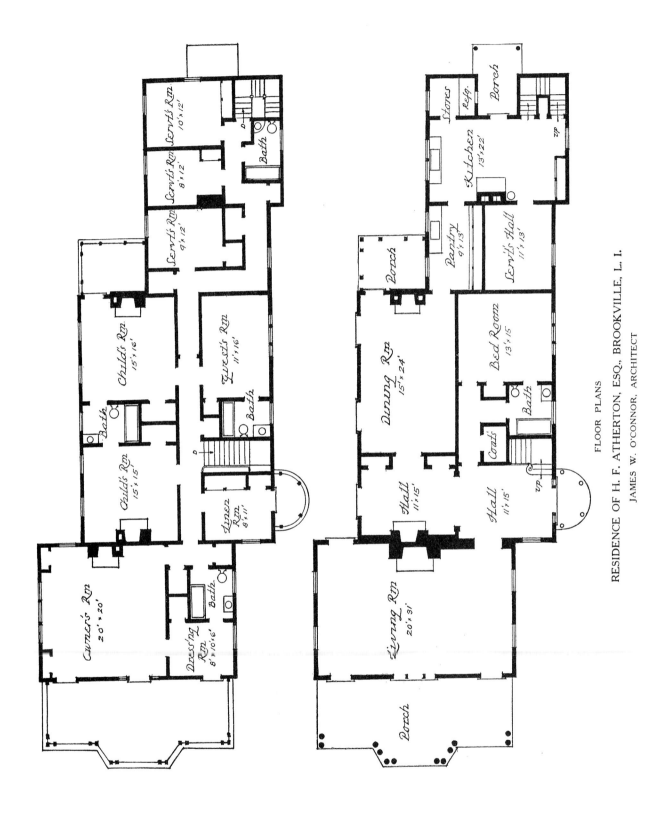

FLOOR PLANS

RESIDENCE OF H. F. ATHERTON, ESQ., BROOKVILLE, L. I.

JAMES W. O'CONNOR, ARCHITECT

ENTRANCE

RESIDENCE OF H. F. ATHERTON, ESQ., BROOKVILLE, L. I.

JAMES W. O'CONNOR, ARCHITECT

DOORWAY

THE HOUSE OF M. A. LEWIS, ESQ., HARTSDALE, N. Y.

DWIGHT JAMES BAUM, ARCHITECT

EXTERIOR
THE HOUSE OF M. A. LEWIS, ESQ., HARTSDALE, N. Y.
DWIGHT JAMES BAUM, ARCHITECT

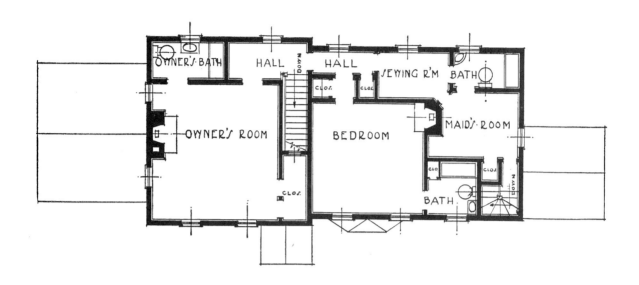

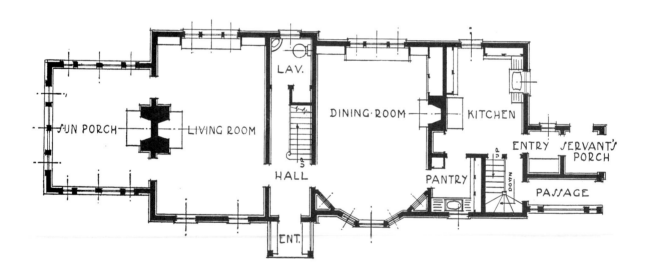

FLOOR PLANS

THE HOUSE OF M. A. LEWIS, ESQ., HARTSDALE, N. Y.

DWIGHT JAMES BAUM, ARCHITECT

VIEW FROM THE NORTH EAST

RESIDENCE OF MR. ELLIS Y. BROWN, JR., DOWNINGTOWN, PA.

MELLOR, MEIGS AND HOWE, ARCHITECTS

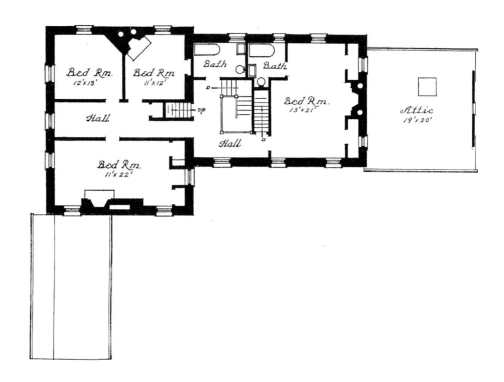

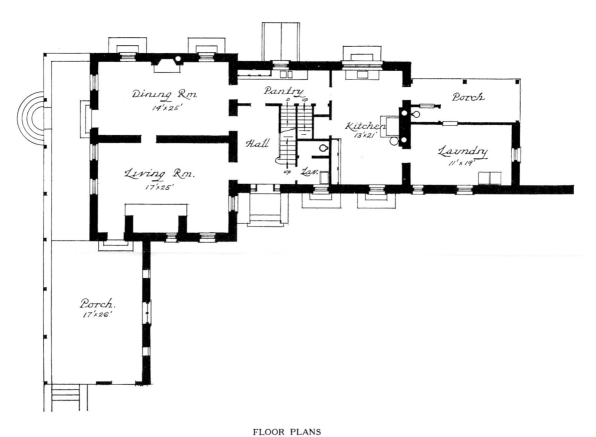

FLOOR PLANS

RESIDENCE OF MR. ELLIS Y. BROWN, JR., DOWNINGTOWN, PA.

MELLOR, MEIGS AND HOWE, ARCHITECTS

EAST ELEVATION

RESIDENCE OF MR. ELLIS Y. BROWN, JR., DOWNINGTOWN, PA.

MELLOR, MEIGS AND HOWE, ARCHITECTS

FRONT DOOR
RESIDENCE OF MR. ELLIS Y. BROWN, JR., DOWNINGTOWN, PA.
MELLOR, MEIGS AND HOWE, ARCHITECTS

DINING ROOM

RESIDENCE OF MR. ELLIS Y. BROWN, JR., DOWNINGTOWN, PA.

MELLOR, MEIGS AND HOWE, ARCHITECTS

VIEW OF LIVING ROOM FROM DINING ROOM

RESIDENCE OF MR. ELLIS Y. BROWN, JR., DOWNINGTOWN, PA.

MELLOR, MEIGS AND HOWE, ARCHITECTS

GARDEN ENTRANCE

ENTRANCE FRONT

THE HOUSE OF HARVEY S. LADEW, ESQ., BROOKVILLE, L. I.

JAMES W. O'CONNOR, ARCHITECT

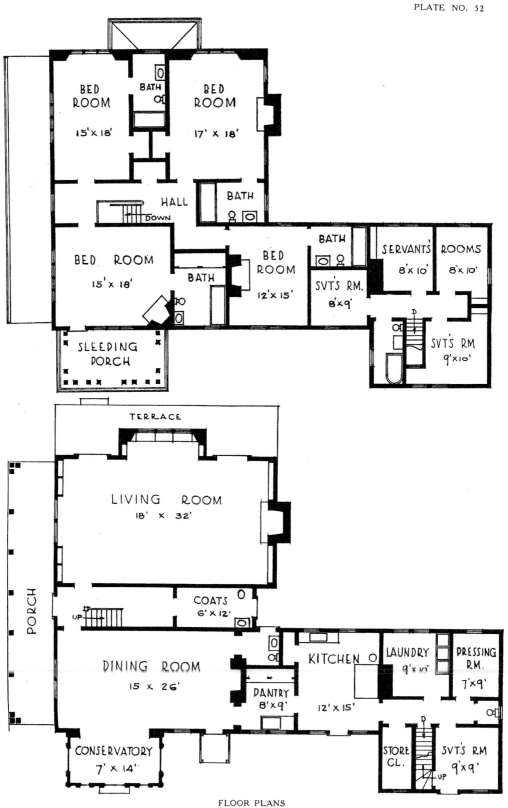

FLOOR PLANS

THE HOUSE OF HARVEY S. LADEW, ESQ., BROOKVILLE, L. I.

JAMES W. O'CONNOR, ARCHITECT

THE DINING ROOM

THE HOUSE OF HARVEY S. LADEW, ESQ., BROOKVILLE, L. I.

JAMES W. O'CONNOR, ARCHITECT

LIVING ROOM

A BED ROOM

THE HOUSE OF HARVEY S. LADEW, ESQ., BROOKVILLE, L. I.

JAMES W. O'CONNOR, ARCHITECT

ENTRANCE FRONT

THE HOUSE OF MISS E. A. WATSON, WHITE PLAINS, N. Y.

DELANO AND ALDRICH, ARCHITECTS

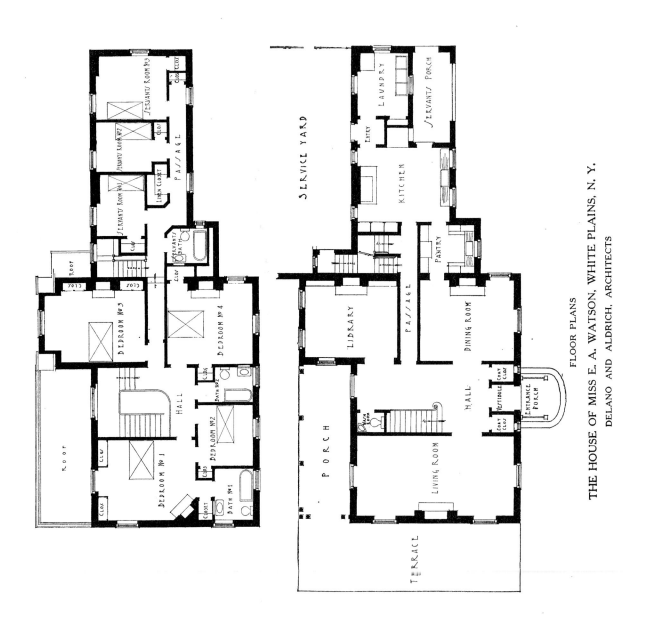

FLOOR PLANS

THE HOUSE OF MISS E. A. WATSON, WHITE PLAINS, N. Y.

DELANO AND ALDRICH, ARCHITECTS

GARDEN FRONT

THE HOUSE OF MISS E. A. WATSON, WHITE PLAINS, N. Y.

DELANO AND ALDRICH, ARCHITECTS

EXTERIOR

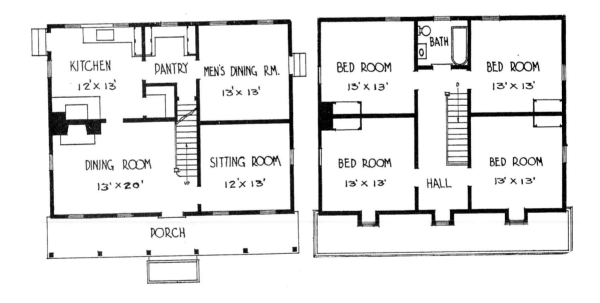

FLOOR PLANS

FARMER'S COTTAGE, ESTATE OF GEORGE S. BREWSTER, ESQ.,

BROOKVILLE, L. I.

ALFRED HOPKINS AND CHARLES S. KEEFE, ARCHITECTS

ENTRANCE SIDE

HOUSE FOR THE MORRIS ESTATE, OVERBROOK, PA.

MELLOR, MEIGS AND HOWE, ARCHITECTS

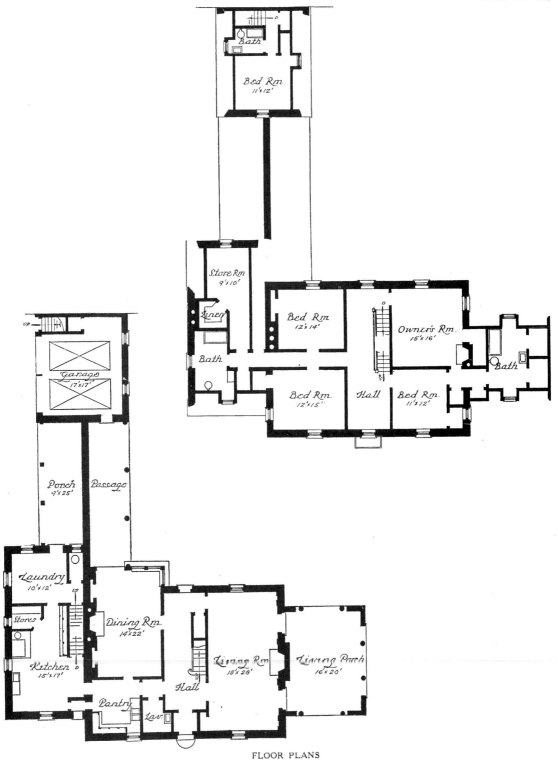

FLOOR PLANS

HOUSE FOR THE MORRIS ESTATE, OVERBROOK, PA.

MELLOR, MEIGS AND HOWE, ARCHITECTS

ENTRANCE

HOUSE FOR THE MORRIS ESTATE, OVERBROOK, PA.

MELLOR, MEIGS AND HOWE, ARCHITECTS

GARDEN SIDE

HOUSE FOR THE MORRIS ESTATE, OVERBROOK, PA.

MELLOR, MEIGS AND HOWE, ARCHITECTS

EXTERIOR

HOUSE FOR WALTER C. BAYLIES, ESQ., TAUNTON, MASS.

PARKER, THOMAS AND RICE, ARCHITECTS

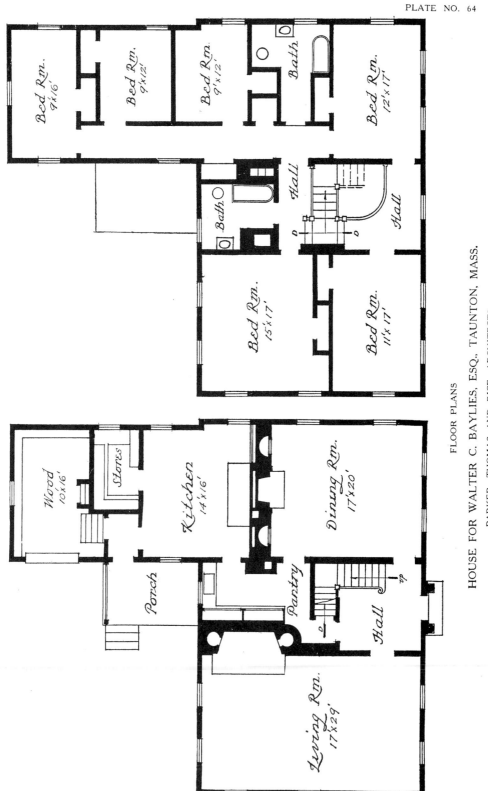

FLOOR PLANS

HOUSE FOR WALTER C. BAYLIES, ESQ., TAUNTON, MASS.

PARKER, THOMAS AND RICE, ARCHITECTS

ENTRANCE DOOR

HOUSE FOR WALTER C. BAYLIES, ESQ., TAUNTON, MASS.

PARKER, THOMAS AND RICE, ARCHITECTS

DINING ROOM

HOUSE FOR WALTER C. BAYLIES, ESQ., TAUNTON, MASS.

PARKER, THOMAS AND RICE, ARCHITECTS

VIEW FROM ROAD

HOUSE OF P. R. JAMESON, ESQ., ROCHESTER, N. Y.

CLEMENT R. NEWKIRK, ARCHITECT OF BAGG AND NEWKIRK

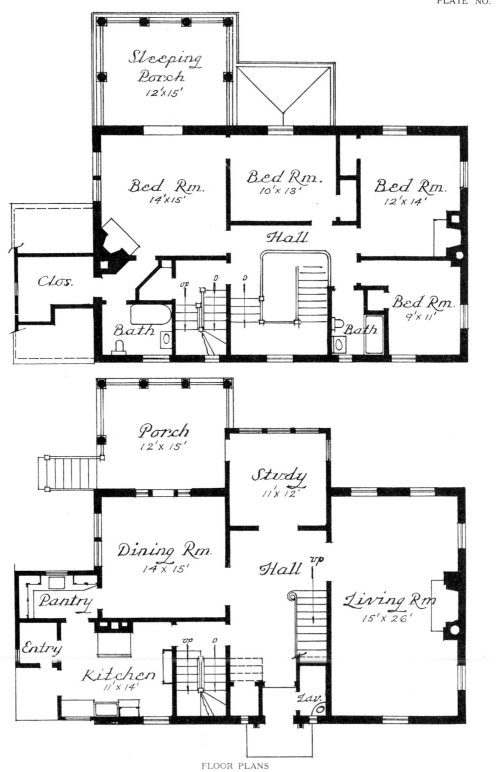

Sleeping Porch
12'x15'

Bed Rm.
14'x15'

Bed Rm.
10'x13'

Bed Rm.
12'x14'

Hall

Clos.

Bath

up

Bath

Bed Rm.
9'x11'

Porch
12'x15'

Study
11'x12'

Dining Rm.
14'x15'

Hall up

Living Rm
15'x26'

Pantry

Entry

Kitchen
11'x14'

up

Lav.

FLOOR PLANS

HOUSE OF P. R. JAMESON, ESQ., ROCHESTER, N. Y.

CLEMENT R. NEWKIRK, ARCHITECT OF BAGG AND NEWKIRK

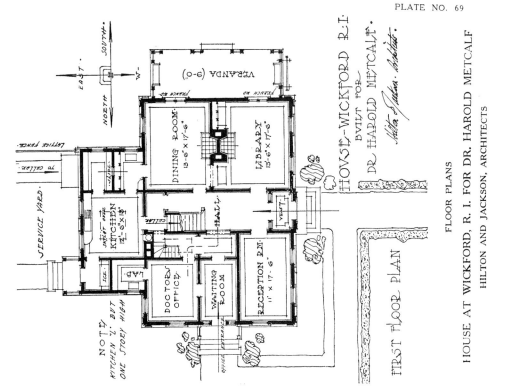

FLOOR PLANS

HOUSE AT WICKFORD, R. I. FOR DR. HAROLD METCALF

HILTON AND JACKSON, ARCHITECTS

ENTRANCE

EXTERIOR
HOUSE AT WICKFORD, R. I. FOR DR. HAROLD METCALF
HILTON AND JACKSON, ARCHITECTS

ENTRANCE FRONT

COTTAGE ON ESTATE OF WM. CHATTIN WETHERILL, ESQ.,

LAVEROCK, PA.

JOHN GRAHAM, JR., ARCHITECT

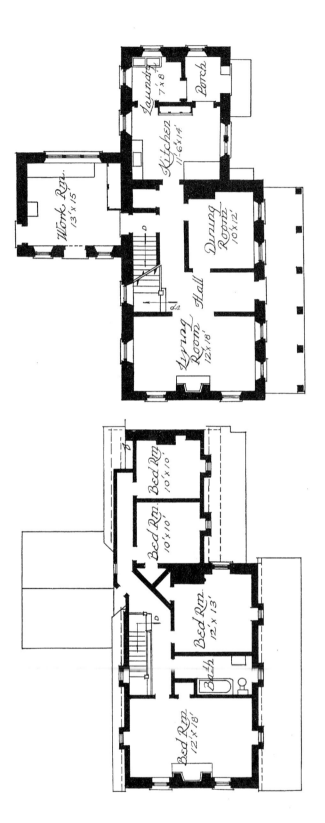

FLOOR PLANS

COTTAGE ON ESTATE OF WM. CHATTIN WETHERILL, ESQ.,

LAVEROCK, PA.

JOHN GRAHAM, JR., ARCHITECT

VIEW AT REAR
COTTAGE ON ESTATE OF WM. CHATTIN WETHERILL, ESQ.,
LAVEROCK, PA.
JOHN GRAHAM, JR., ARCHITECT

PORCH

COTTAGE ON ESTATE OF WM. CHATTIN WETHERILL, ESQ.,

LAVEROCK, PA.

JOHN GRAHAM, JR., ARCHITECT

STREET FRONT
HOUSE OF MR. ROBERT FEIN, RIVERDALE, N. Y.
DWIGHT JAMES BAUM, ARCHITECT

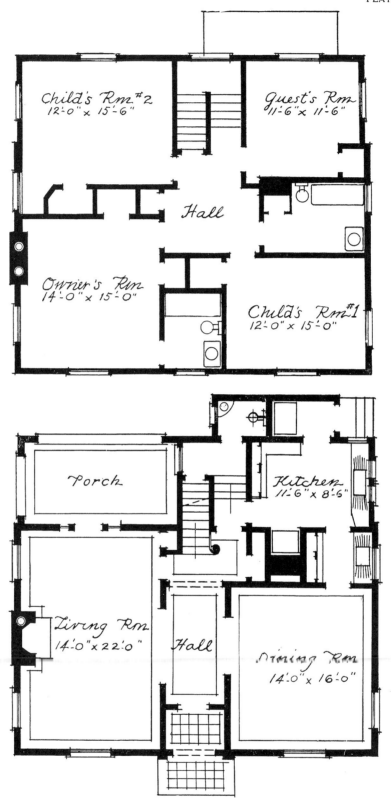

FLOOR PLANS

HOUSE OF MR. ROBERT FEIN, RIVERDALE, N. Y.

DWIGHT JAMES BAUM, ARCHITECT

ENTRANCE DOOR

HOUSE OF MR. ROBERT FEIN, RIVERDALE, N. Y.

DWIGHT JAMES BAUM, ARCHITECT

DETAIL
HOUSE OF MR. ROBERT FEIN, RIVERDALE, N. Y.
DWIGHT JAMES BAUM, ARCHITECT

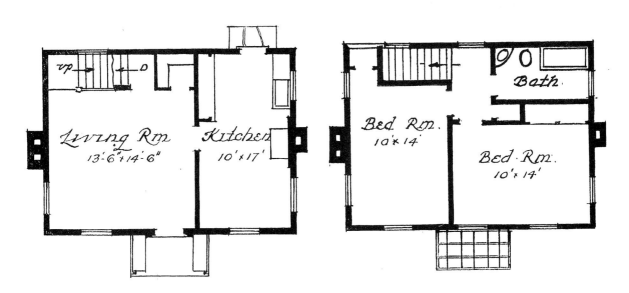

EXTERIOR AND FLOOR PLANS

COTTAGE ON ESTATE OF ANDREW V. STOUT, ESQ., RED BANK, N. J.

JOHN RUSSELL POPE, ARCHITECT

COTTAGE DOORWAY

COTTAGE ON ESTATE OF ANDREW V. STOUT, ESQ., RED BANK, N. J.

JOHN RUSSELL POPE, ARCHITECT

EXTERIOR

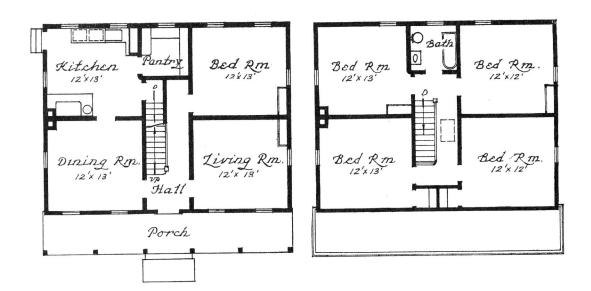

FLOOR PLANS

SUPT'S COTTAGE ESTATE OF GLENN STEWART, ESQ.,

LOCUST VALLEY, L. I.

ALFRED HOPKINS AND CHARLES S. KEEFE, ARCHITECTS

EXTERIOR

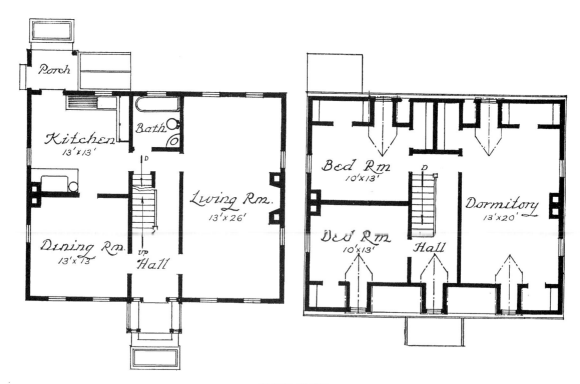

FLOOR PLANS

GARDENER'S COTTAGE FOR ADOLPH MOLLENHAUER, ESQ.,

BAY SHORE, L. I.

ALFRED HOPKINS AND CHARLES S. KEEFE, ARCHITECTS

GEORGIAN HOUSES

ENTRANCE DOOR

THE COUNTRY HOUSE OF OGDEN MILLS, ESQ., WOODBURY, L. I.

JOHN RUSSELL POPE, ARCHITECT

GARDEN ENTRANCE

THE COUNTRY HOUSE OF OGDEN MILLS, ESQ., WOODBURY, L. I.

JOHN RUSSELL POPE, ARCHITECT

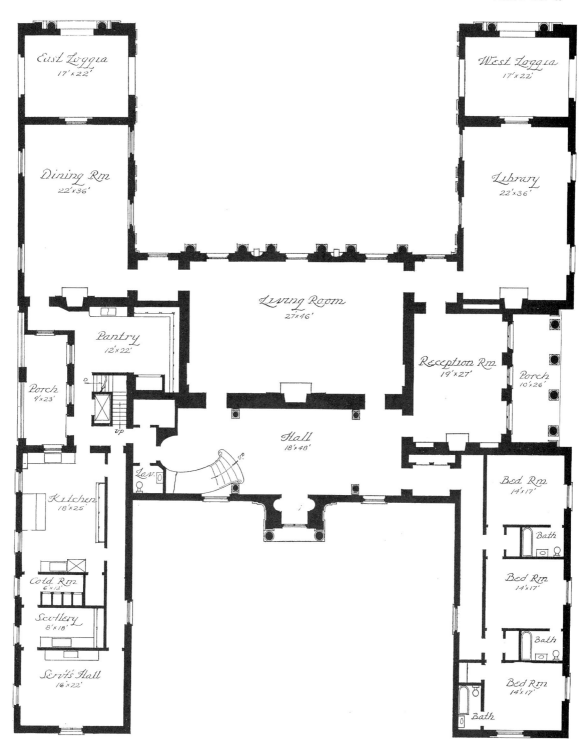

FLOOR PLANS

THE COUNTRY HOUSE OF OGDEN MILLS, ESQ., WOODBURY, L. I.

JOHN RUSSELL POPE, ARCHITECT

GARDEN FRONT

THE COUNTRY HOUSE OF OGDEN MILLS, ESQ., WOODBURY, L. I.

JOHN RUSSELL POPE, ARCHITECT

LOGGIA

THE COUNTRY HOUSE OF OGDEN MILLS, ESQ., WOODBURY, L. I.

JOHN RUSSELL POPE, ARCHITECT

GARDEN FRONT

THE COUNTRY HOUSE OF ARTHUR S. BURDEN, ESQ., JERICHO, L. I.

JOHN RUSSELL POPE, ARCHITECT

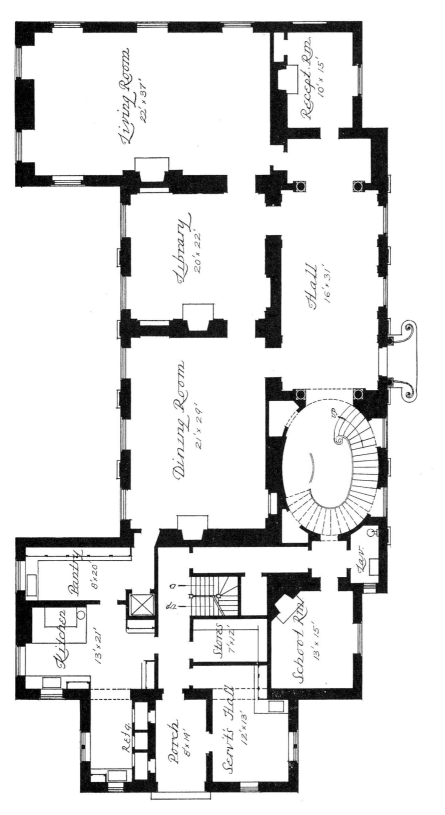

FLOOR PLANS

THE COUNTRY HOUSE OF ARTHUR S. BURDEN, ESQ., JERICHO, L. I.

JOHN RUSSELL POPE, ARCHITECT

ENTRANCE FRONT

THE COUNTRY HOUSE OF ARTHUR S. BURDEN, ESQ., JERICHO, L. I.

JOHN RUSSELL POPE, ARCHITECT

ENTRANCE

THE COUNTRY HOUSE OF ARTHUR S. BURDEN, ESQ., JERICHO, L. I.

JOHN RUSSELL POPE, ARCHITECT

GARDEN STEPS

THE COUNTRY HOUSE OF ARTHUR S. BURDEN, ESQ., JERICHO, L. I.

JOHN RUSSELL POPE, ARCHITECT

THE COUNTRY HOUSE OF ARTHUR S. BURDEN, ESQ., JERICHO, L. I.
JOHN RUSSELL POPE, ARCHITECT

ENTRANCE FRONT

RESIDENCE OF ANDREW V. STOUT, ESQ., RED BANK, N. J.

JOHN RUSSELL POPE, ARCHITECT

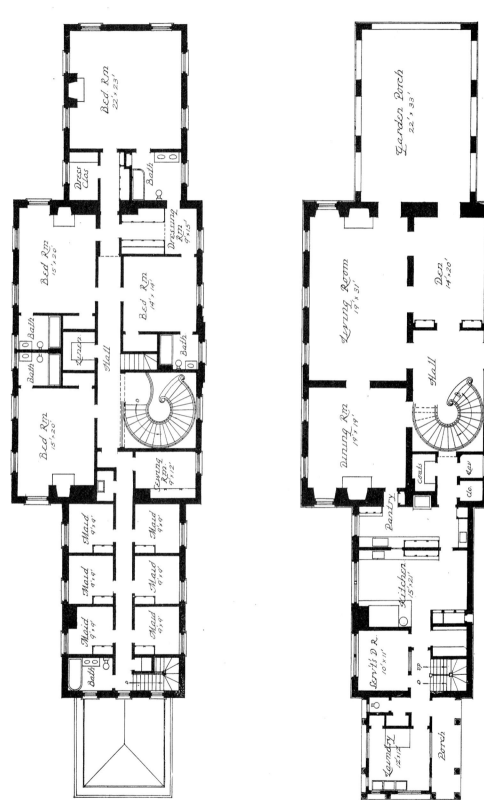

FLOOR PLANS

RESIDENCE OF ANDREW V. STOUT, ESQ., RED BANK, N. J.

JOHN RUSSELL POPE, ARCHITECT

ENTRANCE DOOR

RESIDENCE OF ANDREW V. STOUT, ESQ., RED BANK, N. J.

JOHN RUSSELL POPE, ARCHITECT

THE STAIR HALL
RESIDENCE OF ANDREW V. STOUT, ESQ., RED BANK, N. J.
JOHN RUSSELL POPE, ARCHITECT

LIVING ROOM FIRE PLACE

RESIDENCE OF ANDREW V. STOUT, ESQ., RED BANK, N. J.

JOHN RUSSELL POPE, ARCHITECT

DINING ROOM FIRE PLACE

RESIDENCE OF ANDREW V. STOUT, ESQ., RED BANK, N. J.

JOHN RUSSELL POPE, ARCHITECT

ENTRANCE

RESIDENCE OF JAMES SWAN FRICK, ESQ., GUILFORD, BALTIMORE, MD.

JOHN RUSSELL POPE, ARCHITECT

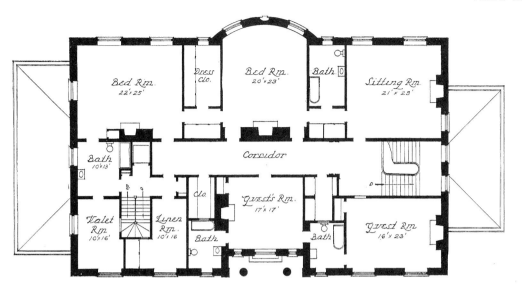

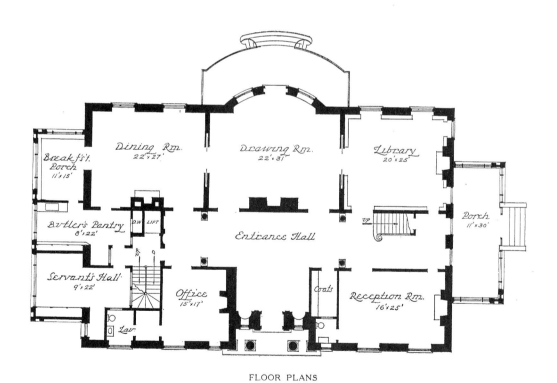

FLOOR PLANS

RESIDENCE OF JAMES SWAN FRICK, ESQ., GUILFORD, BALTIMORE, MD.

JOHN RUSSELL POPE, ARCHITECT

GARDEN FRONT

RESIDENCE OF JAMES SWAN FRICK, ESQ., GUILFORD, BALTIMORE, MD.

JOHN RUSSELL POPE, ARCHITECT

HALLWAY

RESIDENCE OF JAMES SWAN FRICK, ESQ., GUILFORD, BALTIMORE, MD.

JOHN RUSSELL POPE, ARCHITECT

THE STAIR HALL
RESIDENCE OF JAMES SWAN FRICK, ESQ., GUILFORD, BALTIMORE, MD.
JOHN RUSSELL POPE, ARCHITECT

THE LIBRARY
RESIDENCE OF JAMES SWAN FRICK, ESQ., GUILFORD, BALTIMORE, MD.
JOHN RUSSELL POPE, ARCHITECT

ENTRANCE COURT

THE RESIDENCE OF W. F. HENCKEN, ESQ., GREENWICH, CONN.

JOHN RUSSELL POPE, ARCHITECT

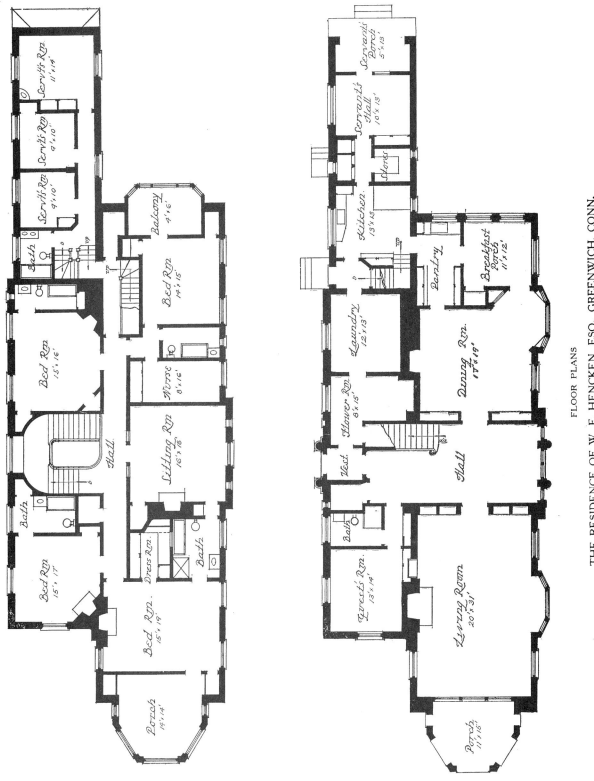

FLOOR PLANS

THE RESIDENCE OF W. F. HENCKEN, ESQ., GREENWICH, CONN.

JOHN RUSSELL POPE, ARCHITECT

GARDEN FRONT

THE RESIDENCE OF W. F. HENCKEN, ESQ., GREENWICH, CONN.

JOHN RUSSELL POPE, ARCHITECT

INTERIOR DOORWAY
THE RESIDENCE OF W. F. HENCKEN, ESQ., GREENWICH, CONN.
JOHN RUSSELL POPE, ARCHITECT

LIVING ROOM FIRE PLACE
THE RESIDENCE OF W. F. HENCKEN, ESQ., GREENWICH, CONN,
JOHN RUSSELL POPE, ARCHITECT

LIVING ROOM

THE RESIDENCE OF W. F. HENCKEN, ESQ., GREENWICH, CONN.

JOHN RUSSELL POPE, ARCHITECT

VIEW OF FORE COURT

HOUSE OF ORMSBY M. MITCHEL, ESQ, RYE, N. Y.

MOTT B. SCHMIDT, ARCHITECT

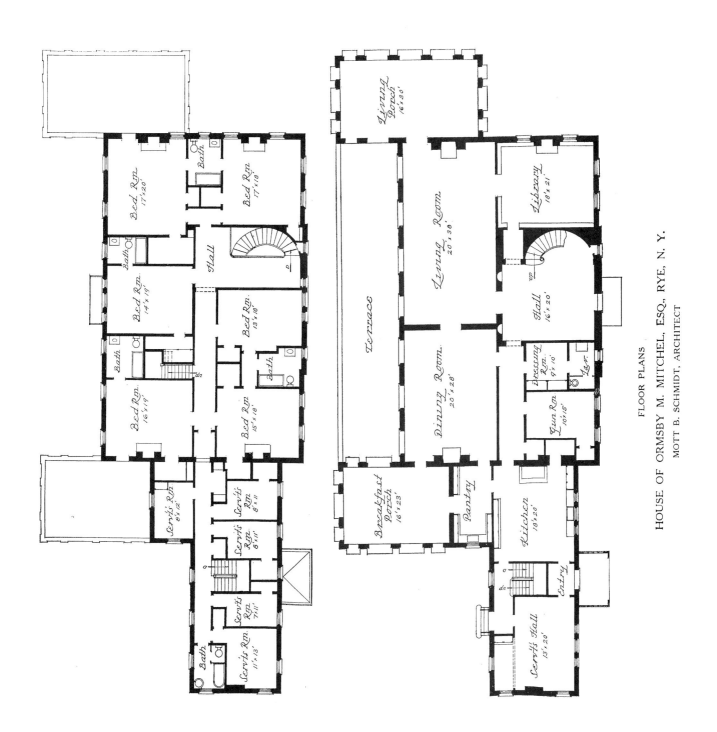

FLOOR PLANS

HOUSE OF ORMSBY M. MITCHEL, ESQ., RYE, N. Y.

MOTT B. SCHMIDT, ARCHITECT

DETAIL OF SUN ROOM
HOUSE OF ORMSBY M. MITCHEL, ESQ., RYE, N. Y.
MOTT B. SCHMIDT, ARCHITECT

POOL IN GARDEN

HOUSE OF ORMSBY M. MITCHEL, ESQ., RYE, N. Y.

MOTT B. SCHMIDT, ARCHITECT

LIVING ROOM

HOUSE OF ORMSBY M. MITCHEL, ESQ., RYE, N. Y.

MOTT B. SCHMIDT, ARCHITECT

DETAIL OF LIBRARY MANTEL

HOUSE OF ORMSBY M. MITCHEL, ESQ., RYE, N. Y.

MOTT B. SCHMIDT, ARCHITECT

ENTRANCE DOOR

THE WILLIAM A. DIXSON HOUSE, GUILFORD, BALTIMORE, MD.

LAURENCE HALL FOWLER, ARCHITECT

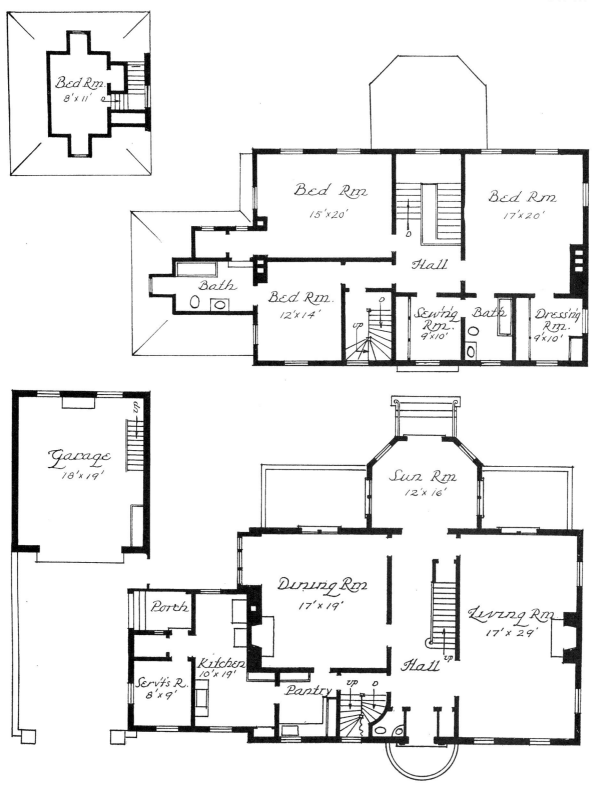

FLOOR PLANS
THE WILLIAM A. DIXSON HOUSE, GUILFORD, BALTIMORE, MD.
LAURENCE HALL FOWLER, ARCHITECT

ENTRANCE FRONT

THE WILLIAM A. DIXSON HOUSE, GUILFORD, BALTIMORE, MD.

LAURENCE HALL FOWLER, ARCHITECT

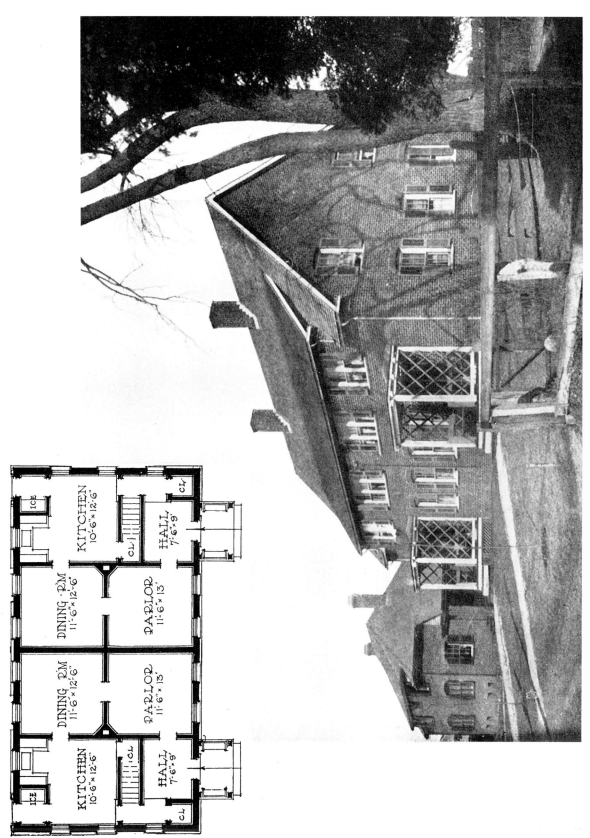

EXTERIOR

TWO SEMI-DETACHED HOUSES FOR GLENLYON DYE WORKS,

PHILLIPSDALE, R. I.

HILTON AND JACKSON, ARCHITECTS

EXTERIOR

HOUSE FOR MR. JAMES A. KINGHORN, PROVIDENCE, R. I.

HILTON AND JACKSON, ARCHITECTS

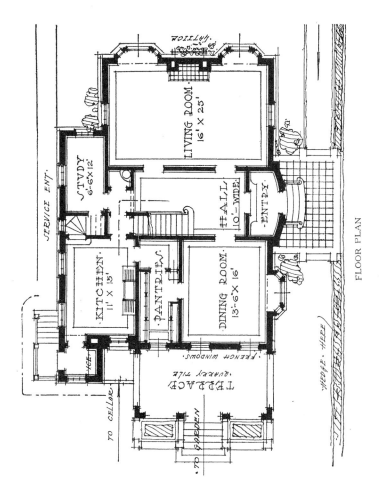

FLOOR PLAN

ENTRANCE

HOUSE FOR MR. JAMES A. KINGHORN, PROVIDENCE, R. I.

HILTON AND JACKSON, ARCHITECTS

ENTRANCE FRONT

COTTAGE ON ESTATE OF MRS. CHARLES O. GATES,

LOCUST VALLEY, L. I.

THEODATE POPE, ARCHITECT

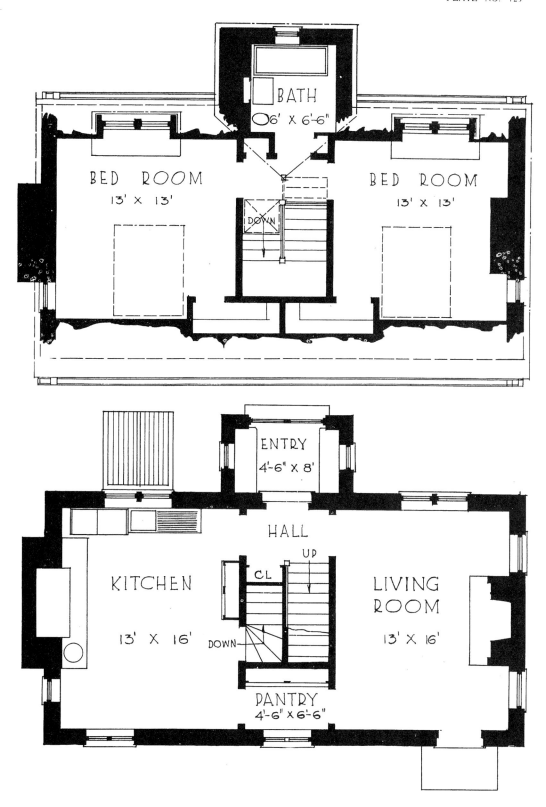

FLOOR PLANS
COTTAGE ON ESTATE OF MRS. CHARLES O. GATES
LOCUST VALLEY, L. I.
THEODATE POPE, ARCHITECT

ITALIAN HOUSES

ENTRANCE

HOUSE OF ERNEST ALLIS, ESQ., LOUISVILLE, KY.

LEWIS COLT ALBRO, ARCHITECT

ENTRANCE FRONT

HOUSE OF ERNEST ALLIS, ESQ., LOUISVILLE, KY.

LEWIS COLT ALBRO. ARCHITECT

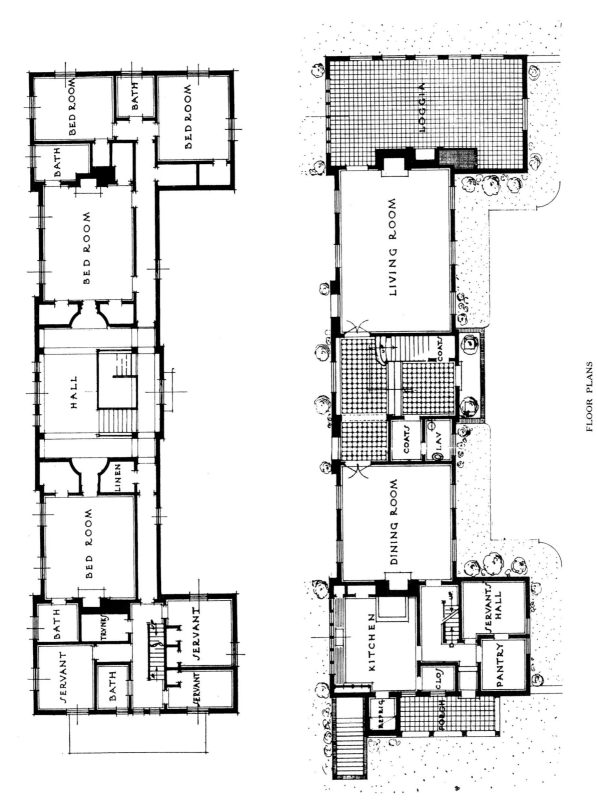

FLOOR PLANS

HOUSE OF ERNEST ALLIS, ESQ., LOUISVILLE, KY.

LEWIS COLT ALBRO, ARCHITECT

FRONT ELEVATION

HOUSE OF HARVEY WARREN, ESQ. FOREST HILLS, L. I.

WM. LAWRENCE BOTTOMLEY, ARCHITECT

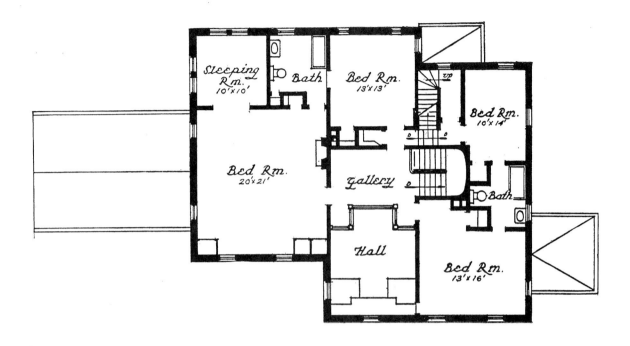

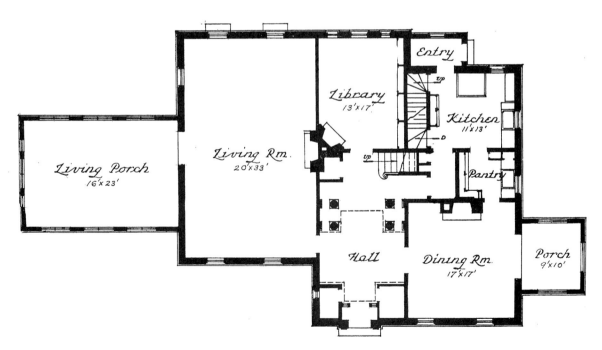

FLOOR PLANS

HOUSE OF HARVEY WARREN, ESQ., FOREST HILLS, L. I.

WM. LAWRENCE BOTTOMLEY, ARCHITECT

ENTRANCE DOORWAY

HOUSE OF HARVEY WARREN, ESQ., FOREST HILLS, L. I.

WM. LAWRENCE BOTTOMLEY, ARCHITECT

DETAIL OF PORCH
HOUSE OF HARVEY WARREN, ESQ., FOREST HILLS, L. I.
WM. LAWRENCE BOTTOMLEY, ARCHITECT

EXTERIOR

RESIDENCE OF JUDGE NASH ROCKWOOD, FIELDSTON, N. Y. C.

DWIGHT JAMES BAUM, ARCHITECT

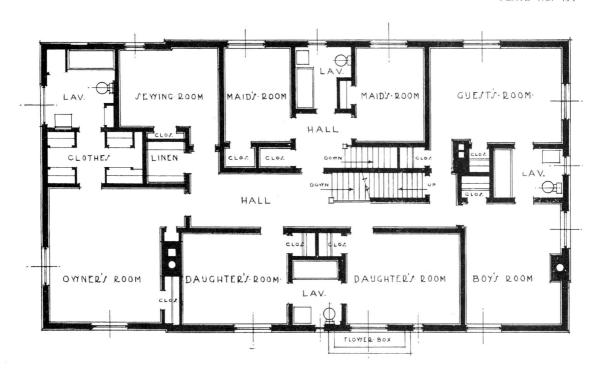

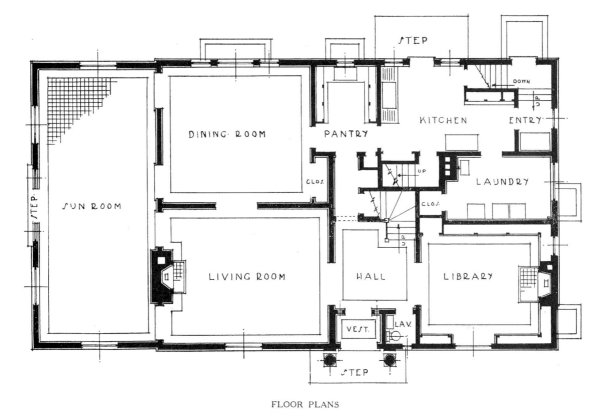

FLOOR PLANS

RESIDENCE OF JUDGE NASH ROCKWOOD, FIELDSTON, N. Y. C.

DWIGHT JAMES BAUM, ARCHITECT

SPANISH HOUSES

ENTRANCE FRONT

THE MAJOR J. H. H. PESHINE, RESIDENCE, SANTA BARBARA, CAL.

MYRON HUNT, ARCHITECT, LOS ANGELES

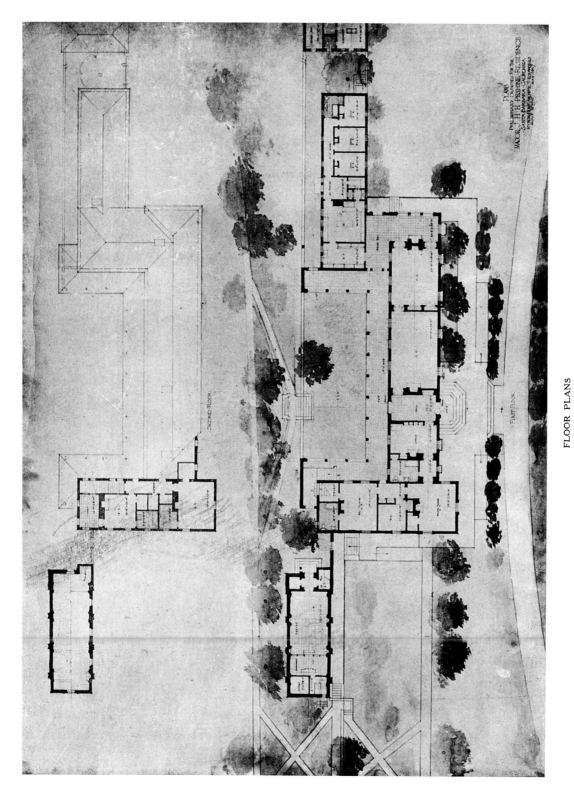

FLOOR PLANS

THE MAJOR J. H. H. PESHINE, RESIDENCE, SANTA BARBARA, CAL.

MYRON HUNT, ARCHITECT, LOS ANGELES

CHAPEL WITH A GLIMPSE OF PATIO

THE MAJOR J. H. H. PESHINE, RESIDENCE, SANTA BARBARA, CAL.

MYRON HUNT, ARCHITECT, LOS ANGELES

THE PATIO

THE MAJOR J. H. H. PESHINE, RESIDENCE, SANTA BARBARA, CAL.

MYRON HUNT, ARCHITECT, LOS ANGELES

COURT AND TERRACE

RESIDENCE OF TOD FORD, JR., ESQ., PASADENA, CAL.

REGINALD D. JOHNSON, ARCHITECT

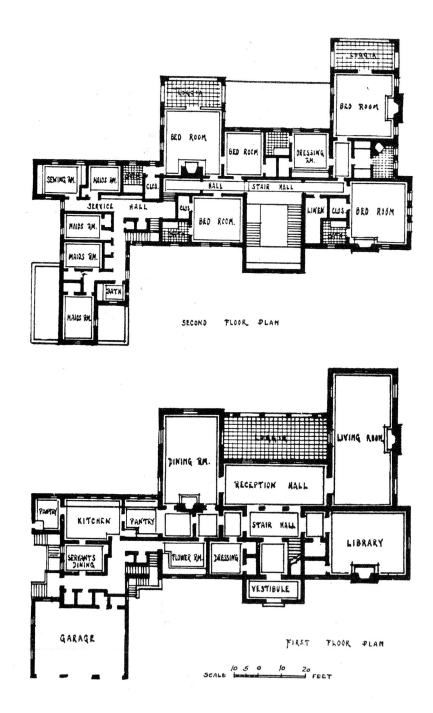

SECOND FLOOR PLAN

FIRST FLOOR PLAN

SCALE |—————| FEET

FLOOR PLANS

RESIDENCE OF TOD FORD, JR., ESQ., PASADENA, CAL.

REGINALD D. JOHNSON, ARCHITECT

ENTRANCE FRONT

RESIDENCE OF TOD FORD, JR., ESQ., PASADENA, CAL.

REGINALD D. JOHNSON, ARCHITECT

EXTERIOR

RESIDENCE OF TOD FORD, JR., ESQ., PASADENA, CAL.

REGINALD D. JOHNSON, ARCHITECT

ENTRANCE THROUGH THE GARDEN

RESIDENCE OF T. R. COFFIN, ESQ., SAN MARINO, CAL.

REGINALD D. JOHNSON, ARCHITECT

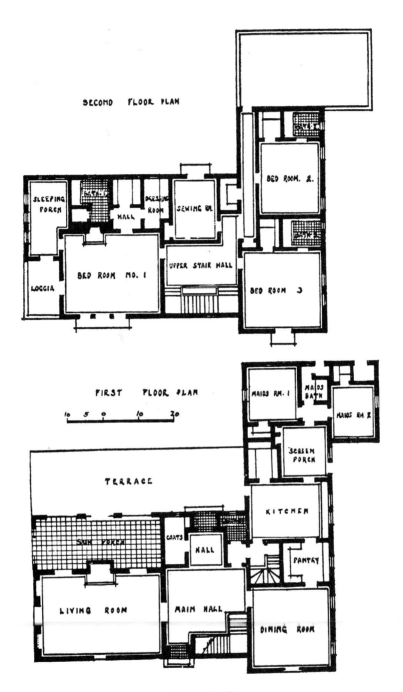

FLOOR PLANS

RESIDENCE OF T. R. COFFIN, ESQ., SAN MARINO, CAL.

REGINALD D. JOHNSON, ARCHITECT

ENTRANCE SIDE

RESIDENCE AT SANTA BARBARA, CAL., OF

GEORGE WASHINGTON SMITH

GEORGE WASHINGTON SMITH, ARCHITECT

THE GARDEN FRONT

RESIDENCE AT SANTA BARBARA, CAL., OF

GEORGE WASHINGTON SMITH

GEORGE WASHINGTON SMITH, ARCHITECT

DRAWING ROOM

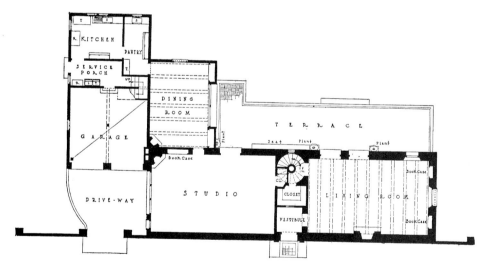

FIRST FLOOR PLAN

FIRST FLOOR PLAN

RESIDENCE AT SANTA BARBARA, CAL., OF
GEORGE WASHINGTON SMITH
GEORGE WASHINGTON SMITH, ARCHITECT

DRAWING ROOM

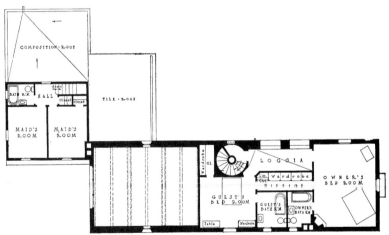

SECOND FLOOR PLAN

SECOND FLOOR PLAN

RESIDENCE AT SANTA BARBARA, CAL., OF
GEORGE WASHINGTON SMITH
GEORGE WASHINGTON SMITH, ARCHITECT

FRENCH HOUSES

FRONT ELEVATION

RESIDENCE OF MR. AND MRS. WILLIAM EVANS, GREENWICH, CONN.

J. E. R. CARPENTER AND WALTER D. BLAIR ASSOC. ARCHITECTS

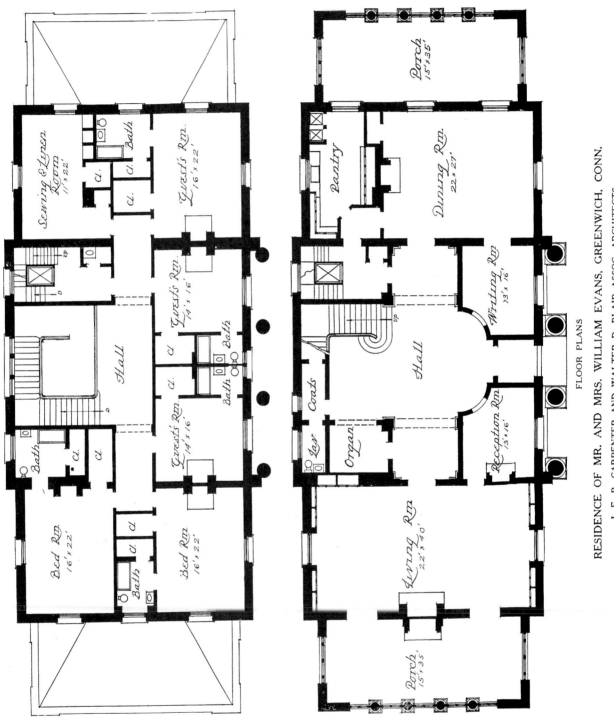

FLOOR PLANS

RESIDENCE OF MR. AND MRS. WILLIAM EVANS, GREENWICH, CONN.

J. E. R. CARPENTER AND WALTER D. BLAIR ASSOC. ARCHITECTS

VIEW OF LIVING ROOM INTO HALL

RESIDENCE OF MR. AND MRS. WILLIAM EVANS, GREENWICH, CONN.

J. E. R. CARPENTER AND WALTER D. BLAIR ASSOC. ARCHITECTS

SOUTH PORCH

RESIDENCE OF MR. AND MRS. WILLIAM EVANS, GREENWICH, CONN.

J. E. R. CARPENTER AND WALTER D. BLAIR ASSOC. ARCHITECTS

VIEW OF DINING ROOM

RESIDENCE OF MR. AND MRS. WILLIAM EVANS, GREENWICH, CONN.

J. E. R. CARPENTER AND WALTER D. BLAIR ASSOC. ARCHITECTS

DETAIL OF DINING ROOM

RESIDENCE OF MR. AND MRS. WILLIAM EVANS, GREENWICH, CONN.

J. E. R. CARPENTER AND WALTER D. BLAIR ASSOC. ARCHITECTS

EXTERIOR

A SMALL HOUSE IN LOS ANGELES, CALIFORNIA
WALTER S. DAVIS, ARCHITECT

FLOOR PLAN

ENGLISH HOUSES

ENTRANCE

THE RESIDENCE OF ALLAN S. LEHMAN, ESQ., TARRYTOWN, N. Y.
JOHN RUSSELL POPE, ARCHITECT

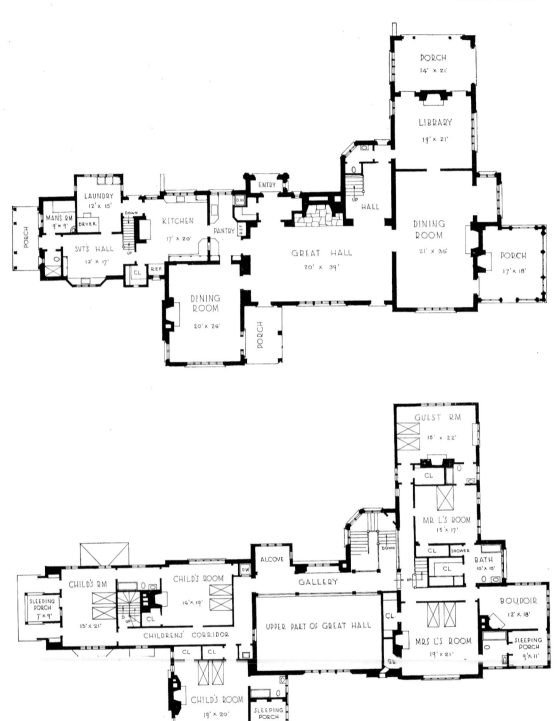

FLOOR PLANS

THE RESIDENCE OF ALLAN S. LEHMAN, ESQ., TARRYTOWN, N. Y.

JOHN RUSSELL POPE, ARCHITECT

SOUTH EAST ELEVATION

THE RESIDENCE OF ALLAN S. LEHMAN, ESQ., TARRYTOWN, N. Y.

JOHN RUSSELL POPE, ARCHITECT

GREAT HALL

THE RESIDENCE OF ALLAN S. LEHMAN, ESQ., TARRYTOWN, N. Y.

JOHN RUSSELL POPE, ARCHITECT

SOUTHWEST VIEW

THE RESIDENCE OF ALLAN S. LEHMAN, ESQ., TARRYTOWN, N. Y.

JOHN RUSSELL POPE, ARCHITECT

LIBRARY

THE RESIDENCE OF ALLAN S. LEHMAN, ESQ., TARRYTOWN, N. Y.

JOHN RUSSELL POPE, ARCHITECT

ENTRANCE COURT

SOUTH ENTRANCE

THE HOUSE OF C. W. MORRIS, ESQ., HAVERFORD, PA.

MELLOR, MEIGS AND HOWE, ARCHITECTS

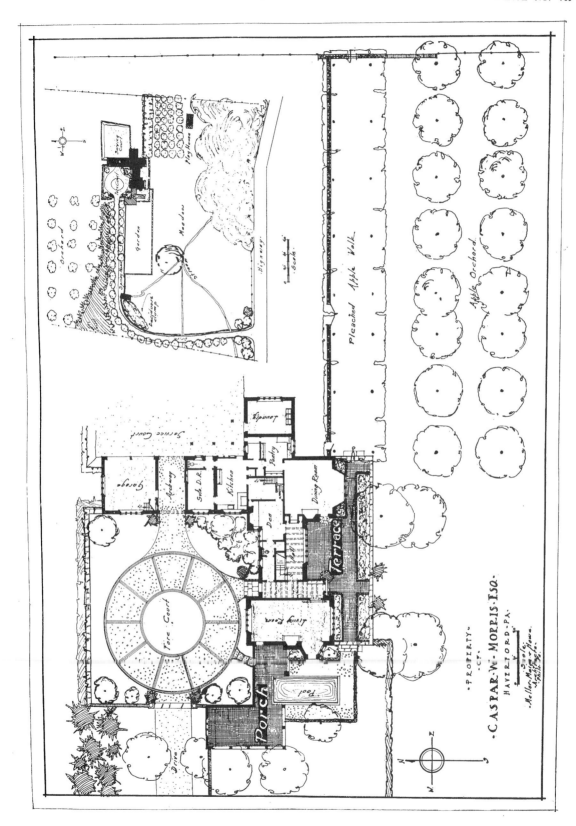

FLOOR PLANS

THE HOUSE OF C. W. MORRIS, ESQ., HAVERFORD, PA.

MELLOR, MEIGS AND HOWE, ARCHITECTS

THE POOL FROM THE PORCH

THE POOL AND THE SLEEPING PORCH

THE HOUSE OF C. W. MORRIS, ESQ., HAVERFORD, PA.

MELLOR, MEIGS AND HOWE, ARCHITECTS

ENTRANCE HALL

SOUTH FACADE FROM FIELDS

THE HOUSE OF C. W. MORRIS, ESQ., HAVERFORD, PA.

MELLOR, MEIGS AND HOWE, ARCHITECTS

THE SERVICE COURT

THE LIVING ROOM

THE HOUSE OF C. W. MORRIS, ESQ., HAVERFORD, PA.

MELLOR, MEIGS AND HOWE, ARCHITECTS

HALLWAY

THE HOUSE OF C. W. MORRIS, ESQ., HAVERFORD, PA.

MELLOR, MEIGS AND HOWE, ARCHITECTS

SOUTH FRONT

HOUSE OF MR. GEORGE ARENTS, JR., RYE, N. Y.

LEWIS COLT ALBRO, ARCHITECT

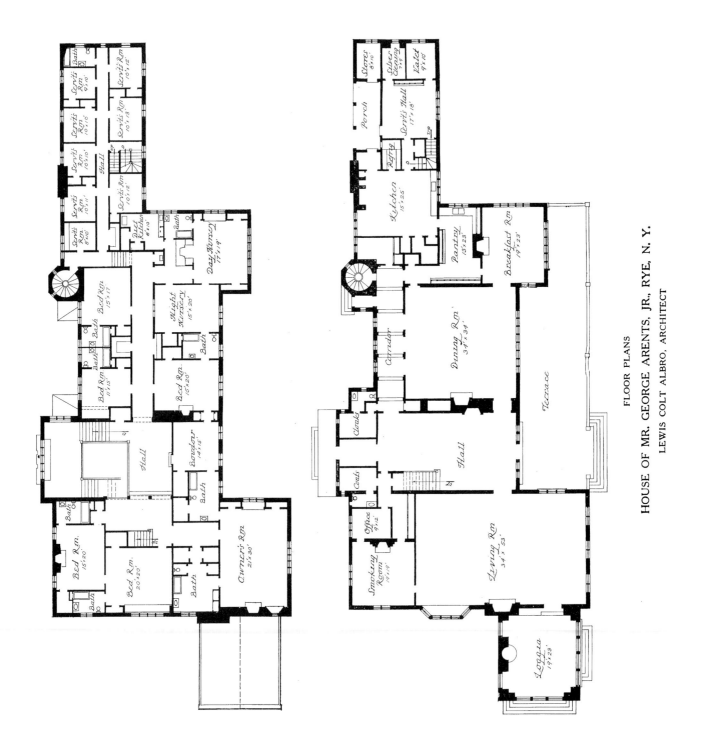

FLOOR PLANS

HOUSE OF MR. GEORGE ARENTS, JR., RYE, N. Y.

LEWIS COLT ALBRO, ARCHITECT

ENTRANCE

HOUSE OF MR. GEORGE ARENTS, JR., RYE, N. Y.

LEWIS COLT ALBRO, ARCHITECT

SOUTH TERRACE

HOUSE OF MR. GEORGE ARENTS, JR., RYE, N. Y.

LEWIS COLT ALBRO ARCHITECT

GARDEN POOL AND SUN PARLOR
HOUSE OF MR. GEORGE ARENTS, JR., RYE, N. Y.
LEWIS COLT ALBRO, ARCHITECT

SOUTH ELEVATION FROM GARDEN

HOUSE OF MR. GEORGE ARENTS, JR., RYE, N. Y.

LEWIS COLT ALBRO, ARCHITECT

THE HOUSE FROM THE HIGHWAY

RESIDENCE FOR FRANCIS S. MC-ILHENNY, ESQ., CHESTNUT HILL, PA.

MELLOR, MEIGS AND HOWE, ARCHITECTS

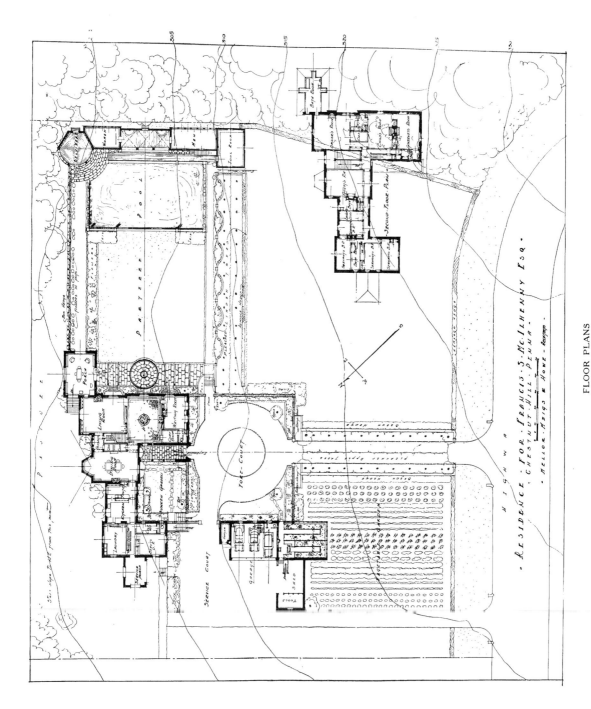

FLOOR PLANS

RESIDENCE FOR FRANCIS S. MC-ILHENNY, ESQ., CHESTNUT HILL, PA.

MELLOR, MEIGS AND HOWE, ARCHITECTS

MAIN HALL
RESIDENCE FOR FRANCIS S. MC-ILHENNY, ESQ., CHESTNUT HILL, PA.
MELLOR, MEIGS AND HOWE, ARCHITECTS

ENTRANCE LOGGIA

RESIDENCE FOR FRANCIS S. MC-ILHENNY, ESQ., CHESTNUT HILL, PA.

MELLOR, MEIGS AND HOWE, ARCHITECTS

THE ENTRANCE FRONT

THE HOUSE OF JOSEPH AND ELIZABETH CHAMBERLAIN

MIDDLEBURY, CONN.

THEODATE POPE, ARCHITECT

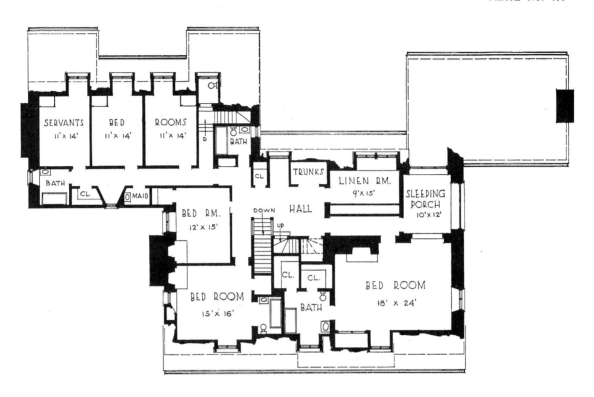

FLOOR PLANS

THE HOUSE OF JOSEPH AND ELIZABETH CHAMBERLAIN,

MIDDLEBURY, CONN.

THEODATE POPE, ARCHITECT

VIEW FROM THE GARDEN

THE HOUSE OF JOSEPH AND ELIZABETH CHAMBERLAIN

MIDDLEBURY, CONN.

THEODATE POPE, ARCHITECT

VIEW THROUGH HALL
THE HOUSE OF JOSEPH AND ELIZABETH CHAMBERLAIN
MIDDLEBURY, CONN.
THEODATE POPE, ARCHITECT

EXTERIOR

THE HOUSE OF JEROME MENDLESON, ESQ., ALBANY, N. Y.

LEWIS COLT ALBRO, ARCHITECT

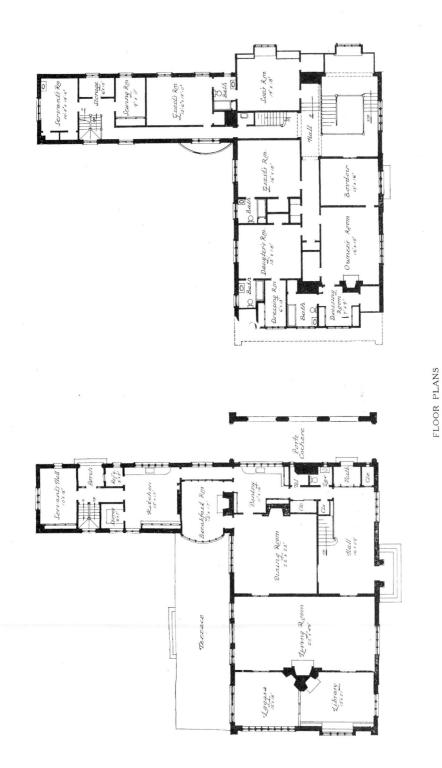

FLOOR PLANS

THE HOUSE OF JEROME MENDLESON, ESQ., ALBANY, N. Y.

LEWIS COLT ALBRO, ARCHITECT

ENTRANCE

THE HOUSE OF JEROME MENDLESON, ESQ., ALBANY, N. Y.

LEWIS COLT ALBRO, ARCHITECT

FRONT ELEVATION

COTTAGE ON ESTATE OF MR. GEORGE ARENTS, JR., RYE, N. Y.

LEWIS COLT ALBRO, ARCHITECT

ENTRANCE FRONT

HOUSE OF ANDREW J. THOMAS, ESQ., SCARSDALE, N. Y.

ANDREW J. THOMAS, ARCHITECT

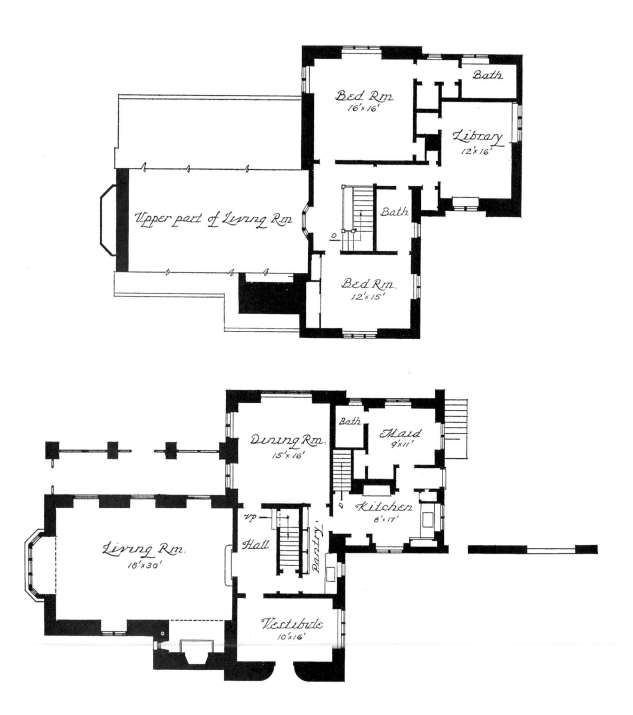

FLOOR PLANS
HOUSE OF ANDREW J. THOMAS, ESQ., SCARSDALE, N. Y.
ANDREW J. THOMAS, ARCHITECT

VIEW FROM GARDEN

HOUSE OF ANDREW J. THOMAS, ESQ., SCARSDALE, N. Y.

ANDREW J. THOMAS, ARCHITECT

THE LIVING ROOM

THE DINING ROOM

HOUSE OF ANDREW J. THOMAS, ESQ., SCARSDALE, N. Y.

ANDREW J. THOMAS, ARCHITECT

ENTRANCE
THE STUDIO HOME OF CHARLES E. CHAMBERS, ESQ.,
RIVERDALE, N. Y.
JULIUS GREGORY, ARCHITECT

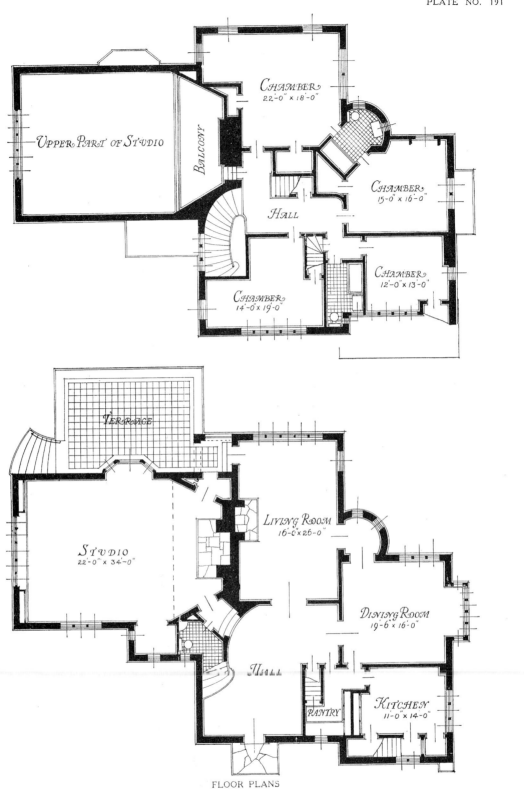

UPPER PART OF STUDIO

BALCONY

CHAMBER
22'-0" x 18'-0"

CHAMBER
15'-0" x 16'-0"

HALL

CHAMBER
12'-0" x 13'-0"

CHAMBER
14'-0" x 19'-0"

TERRACE

STUDIO
22'-0" x 34'-0"

LIVING ROOM
16'-0" x 26'-0"

DINING ROOM
19'-6" x 16'-0"

HALL

PANTRY

KITCHEN
11'-0" x 14'-0"

FLOOR PLANS
THE STUDIO HOME OF CHARLES E. CHAMBERS, ESQ.,
RIVERDALE, N. Y.
JULIUS GREGORY, ARCHITECT

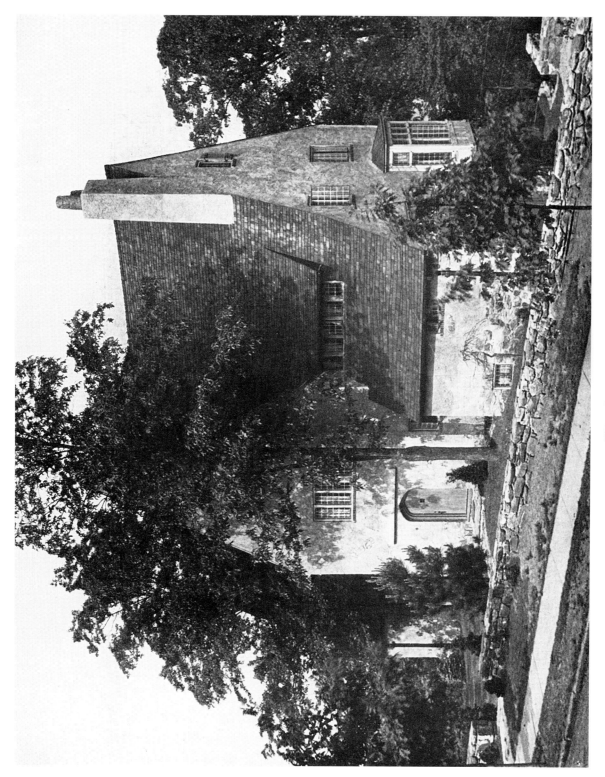

ENTRANCE FRONT
THE STUDIO HOME OF CHARLES E. CHAMBERS, ESQ.,
RIVERDALE, N. Y.
JULIUS GREGORY, ARCHITECT

DINING ROOM

HALL

THE STUDIO HOME OF CHARLES E. CHAMBERS, ESQ.,
RIVERDALE, N. Y.
JULIUS GREGORY, ARCHITECT

INTERIORS

FOYER HALL
RESIDENCE OF MRS. GEORGE B. POST, JR., NEW YORK.
MOTT B. SCHMIDT, ARCHITECT

STAIR HALL
HOUSE OF MR. ROBERT L. WOOD, WHITEMARSH, PA.
JOHN GRAHAM, JR., ARCHITECT

HALLWAY

HAROLD CARHART RESIDENCE, LOCUST VALLEY. L. I.

HOWARD MAJOR, ARCHITECT

HALLWAY
HOUSE OF MR. FRED DANA MARSH, MURAL PAINTER,
NEW ROCHELLE, N. Y.
H. G. MORSE, ARCHITECT

DRAWING ROOM MANTEL
RESIDENCE OF MRS. GEORGE B. POST, JR., NEW YORK.
MOTT B. SCHMIDT, ARCHITECT

LIBRARY MANTEL
RESIDENCE OF MRS. GRENVILLE S. EMMET, NEW YORK
MOTT B. SCHMIDT, ARCHITECT

MANTEL

HUGH LEGARE RESIDENCE, WASHINGTON, D. C.

HOWARD MAJOR, ARCHITECT

MANTEL IN DRAWING ROOM

RESIDENCE OF ALBERT R. WAMPOLE, ESQ., GUILFORD, MD.

MOTT B. SCHMIDT, ARCHITECT

LIVING ROOM

W. T. GRANT RESIDENCE, PELHAM, N. Y.

HOWARD MAJOR, ARCHITECT

LIVING ROOM

HOUSE OF MRS. WM. J. WILCOX, ST. DAVIDS, PA.

MELLOR, MEIGS AND HOWE, ARCHITECT

DINING ROOM

HAROLD CARHART RESIDENCE, LOCUST VALLEY. L. I.

HOWARD MAJOR, ARCHITECT

THE LIVING ROOM

HOUSE OF CHARLES M. HART, PELHAM MANOR, N. Y.

CHARLES M. HART, ARCHITECT

MANTEL IN HALL

HOUSE OF O. L. SCHWENKE, JR., BAY SHORE, L. I.

DWIGHT JAMES BAUM, ARCHITECT

UPPER HALL
COUNTRY HOUSE OF JULES BREUCHAUD, ULSTER CO., N. Y.
MYRON S. TELLER, ARCHITECT

BED ROOM

HOUSE OF CHARLES M. HART, PELHAM MANOR, N. Y.

CHARLES M. HART, ARCHITECT

HALLWAY

HOUSE OF CHARLES M. HART, PELHAM MANOR, N. Y.

CHARLES M. HART, ARCHITECT

HALL
THE DILLON HOUSE, KINGSTON, N. Y.
MYRON S. TELLER, ARCHITECT

LIVING ROOM

BED ROOM

COUNTRY HOUSE OF JULES BREUCHAUD, ULSTER CO., N. Y.

MYRON S. TELLER, ARCHITECT

DINING ROOM
HOUSE OF MR. FRED DANA MARSH, MURAL PAINTER,
NEW ROCHELLE, N. Y.
H. G. MORSE, ARCHITECT

LIVING ROOM IN NORTH WING

HOUSE OF LATHROP BROWN, ESQ., ST. JAMES, LONG ISLAND, N. Y.

PEABODY, WILSON AND BROWN, ARCHITECTS

DOORWAYS

DOORWAY

SAMUEL DWIGHT BREWSTER RESIDENCE, GLEN COVE, L. I.

HOWARD MAJOR, ARCHITECT

DOORWAY

THE HOUSE OF DR. T. J. ABBOTT, CORNWALL-ON-THE-HUDSON, N. Y.

PARKER MORSE HOOPER, ARCHITECT

DOORWAY
WM. B. HESTER RESIDENCE, GLEN COVE, L. I.
HOWARD MAJOR, ARCHITECT

ENTRANCE DOORWAY

WILLIAM BEARD RESIDENCE, GLEN COVE, L. I.

HOWARD MAJOR, ARCHITECT

DOORWAY
J. H. OTTLEY RESIDENCE, GLEN COVE, L. I.
HOWARD MAJOR, ARCHITECT

DOORWAY
HOUSE OF MRS. WM. J. WILCOX, ST. DAVIDS, PA.
MELLOR, MEIGS AND HOWE, ARCHITECTS

Dover Books on Art & Art History

De Re Metallica, Georgius Agricola. One of the most important scientific classics of all time, this 1556 work on mining was the first based on field research and observation and the methods of modern science. 289 authentic Renaissance woodcuts. Translated by Herbert Hoover. Reprint of English (1912) edition. 672pp. 6¾ x 10¾. 60006-8

The Pirotechnia, Vannoccio Biringuccio. History's first clear, comprehensive work on metallurgy, published in 1540, describing in detail the equipment and processes of 16th-century mining, smelting, and metalworking. 94 original woodcuts. Introduction. 507pp. 6⅛ x 9¼. 26134-4

The Art of Botanical Illustration: An Illustrated History, Wilfrid Blunt. Surveys the evolution of botanical illustration from the crude scratchings of paleolithic man down to the highly scientific work of 20th-century illustrators. With 186 magnificent examples, more than 30 in full color. "A classic"–*The Sunday Times* (London). 372pp. 5⅜ x 8¼. 27265-6

Idols Behind Altars: Modern Mexican Art and Its Cultural Roots, Anita Brenner. Critical study ranges from pre-Columbian times through the 20th century to explore Mexico's intrinsic association between art and religion; the role of iconography in Mexican art; and the return to native values. Unabridged reprint of the classic 1929 edition. 118 b/w illustrations. 432pp. 5⅜ x 8½. 42303-4

The Book of Kells, Blanche Cirker (ed.). 32 full-color, full-page plates from the greatest illuminated manuscript of the Middle Ages; painstakingly reproduced from rare facsimile edition. Publisher's Note. Captions. 32pp. 9⅜ x 12¼. 24345-1

Christian and Oriental Philosophy of Art, Ananda K. Coomaraswamy. Nine essays by philosopher-art-historian on symbolism, traditional culture, folk art, ideal portraiture, etc. 146pp. 5⅜ x 8½. 20378-6

Dalí on Modern Art, Salvador Dalí. Influential painter skewers modern art and its practitioners. Outrageous evaluations of Picasso, Cézanne, Turner, and more. 15 renderings of paintings discussed. 44 calligraphic decorations by Dalí. 96pp. 5⅜ x 8½. 29220-7

The Secret Life of Salvador Dalí, Salvador Dalí. One of the most readable autobiographies ever! Superbly illustrated with more than 80 photos of Dalí and his works, and scores of Dalí drawings and sketches. "It is impossible not to admire this painter as writer . . . (Dalí) communicates the snobbishness, self-adoration, comedy, seriousness, fanaticism, in short the concept of life and the total picture of himself he sets out to portray."–*Books.* 432pp. 6½ x 9¼. (Available in U.S. only) 27454-3

Leonardo on Art and the Artist, Leonardo da Vinci (André Chastel, ed.). Systematic grouping of passages of Leonardo's writings concerning painting, with focus on problems of interpretation. More than an anthology, it offers a reconstruction of the underlying meaning of Leonardo's words. Introduction, notes, and bibliographic and reference materials. More than 125 b/w illustrations. 288pp. 9¼ x 7⅜. 42166-X

Leonardo on the Human Body, Leonardo da Vinci. More than 1,200 of Leonardo's anatomical drawings on 215 plates. Leonardo's text, which accompanies the drawings, has been translated into English. 506pp. 8⅜ x 11¾. 24483-0

The Book Before Printing: Ancient, Medieval and Oriental, David Diringer. Rich authoritative study of the book before Gutenberg. Nearly 200 photographic facsimiles of priceless documents. 604pp. 5⅜ x 8½. 24243-9

America's Old Masters: Benjamin West, John Singleton Copley, Charles Willson Peale and Gilbert Stuart, James T. Flexner. Concise biographies evaluate each painter, wellsprings of their art, interplay of native tradition and European influence, and more. 69 halftones. Bibliography. 448pp. 5⅞ x 8¼. 27957-X

Gauguin's Intimate Journals, Paul Gauguin. Revealing documents, reprinted from rare, limited edition, throw much light on the painter's inner life, his tumultuous relationship with van Gogh, evaluations of Degas, Monet, and other artists; hatred of hypocrisy and sham, life in the Marquesas Islands, and much more. 27 full-page illustrations by Gauguin. Preface by Emil Gauguin. 160pp. 6½ x 9¼. 29441-2

The Geometry of Art and Life, Matila Ghyka. Revealing discussion ranging from Plato to modern architecture. 80 plates and 64 figures, including paintings, flowers, shells, etc. 174pp. 5⅜ x 8½. 23542-4

The Life of William Blake, Alexander Gilchrist. First full-length biography (1863) covers Blake's childhood, student years, trial for treason, his "madness," neglect by the public, declining health, and untimely death. Insightful commentary on the poet's works. 40 Blake illustrations. 640pp. 5⅜ x 8½. 40005-0

A Manual of Historic Ornament, Richard Glazier. Hundreds of detailed illustrations depict painted pilasters from Pompeii, early Gothic stone carvings, a detail from a stained glass window in Canterbury Cathedral, and much more. Unabridged reprint of the 6th edition (1948) of *A Manual of Historic Ornament,* originally published in 1899 by B. T. Batsford, Ltd., London. Over 700 b/w illustrations. 16 plates of photographs. x+230pp. 6⅛ x 9¼. 42148-1

The Disasters of War, Francisco Goya. This powerful graphic indictment of war's horrors–inspired by the Peninsular War and the following famine–comprises 80 prints and includes veiled attacks on various people, the Church, and the State. Captions reprinted with English translations. 97pp. 9⅜ x 8¼. 21872-4

Great Drawings of Nudes, Carol Belanger Grafton (ed.). An impressive sampling of life drawings by 45 of the art world's greatest masters displays the styles of figure drawing across five centuries, from Dürer and Michelangelo to Modigliani and Derain. Featured artists include Raphael, Rubens, van Dyck, Hogarth, Constable, Ingres, Gauguin, Matisse, Rodin, and others. Captions. 48pp. 8¼ x 11. 42766-8

Great Self-Portraits, Carol Belanger Grafton (ed.). Unique volume of 45 splendid self-portraits encompasses pen, ink, and charcoal renderings as well as etchings and engravings. Subjects range from such 15th-century artists as da Vinci and Dürer to a host of 19th-century masters: Whistler, Rodin, van Gogh, Beardsley, and many more–Rembrandt, Rubens, Goya, Blake, Pissarro, and numerous others. 45 b/w illustrations. 48pp. 8¼ x 11. 42168-6

Form, Function & Design, Paul Jacques Grillo. One of finest modern analyses of design and its related variables–form, materials, climate, orientation, proportion, and composition. 422 illustrations. 238pp. 8¼ x 11. 20182-1

Hawthorne on Painting, Charles W. Hawthorne. Collected from notes taken by students at famous Cape Cod School; hundreds of direct, personal aperçus, ideas, suggestions. 91pp. 5⅜ x 8½. 20653-X

Modern Mexican Painters, MacKinley Helm. Definitive introduction to art and artists of Mexico during great artistic movements of '20s and '30s. Discussion of Rivera, Orozco, Siqueiros, Galvan, Cantú, Meza, and many others. 95 illustrations. 228pp. 6½ x 9¼. 26028-3

Modern Artists on Art, Second Enlarged Edition, Robert L. Herbert (ed.). Sixteen of the twentieth century's leading artistic innovators talk forcefully about their work–from Albert Gleizes and Jean Metzinger's 1912 presentation of Cubist theory to Henry Moore's comments, three decades later, on sculpture and primitive art. Four essays by Kurt Schwitters, Max Ernst, El Lissitzky, and Fernand Léger. 192pp. 5⅜ x 8½. 41191-5

A History of Engraving and Etching, Arthur M. Hind. British Museum Keeper of Prints offers complete history, from 15th century to 1914: accomplishments, influences, and artistic merit. 111 illustrations. 505pp. 5⅜ x 8½. 20954-7

Art and Geometry, William M. Ivins. Stimulating, controversial study of interrelations of art and mathematics, Greek disservice and contribution. Renaissance perspective, Dürer and math, etc. 123pp. 5⅜ x 8½. 20941-5

Concerning the Spiritual in Art, Wassily Kandinsky. Pioneering work by father of abstract art. Thoughts on color theory and nature of art. Analysis of earlier masters. 12 illustrations. 80pp. of text. 5⅜ x 8½. 23411-8

*Write for **free** Fine Art and Art Instruction Catalog to*
Dover Publications, Inc., Dept. ABI, 31 East 2nd Street, Mineola, NY 11501
*Visit us online at **www.doverpublications.com***

Twentieth-Century Art

FRENCH SATIRICAL DRAWINGS FROM "L'ASSIETTE AU BEURRE," Stanley Appelbaum (ed.). 170 biting, original drawings (8 in full color) from French magazine with an unsurpassed style. Works by Steinlen, Cappiello, Caran d'Ache, Willette, Poulbot, Forain, Vallotton, and Robida–as well as Juan Gris, Jacques Villon, Kees van Dongen, and Frantisek Kupka. 183pp. 9⅜ x 12¼. 23583-1

SIMPLICISSIMUS, edited and translated by Stanley Appelbaum. 180 satirical drawings, 16 in full color, from 1896 to 1926. The 24 artists represented include Grosz, Kley, Pascin, and others. 172pp. 8½ x 12¼. 23099-6

THE VIBRANT METROPOLIS: 88 LITHOGRAPHS, George W. Bellows (selected by Carol Belanger Grafton). Brilliantly executed, richly evocative works by one of the most popular American artists of the early 20th century include *Nude in a Bed, Evening; In the Subway; Dempsey Through the Ropes;* and *Base Hospital,* among others. 96pp. 8⅜ x 11. 42304-2

CHAGALL DRAWINGS: 43 WORKS, Marc Chagall. Superb treasury of images by one of the most distinctive and original artists of the 20th century–from fanciful fiddlers hovering above rooftops to imaginatively conceived depictions of bareback riders and other circus performers. Includes, among other masterworks, *Wounded Soldier, Three Acrobats, Child on a Chair, Nude with a Fan, Peasants in Vitebsk,* and *The Magician.* 48pp. 8¼ x 11. 41222-9

DRAWINGS FOR THE BIBLE, Marc Chagall. 136 works, 24 in full color, depicting Old Testament subjects. Captions cite the biblical sources of each drawing. Reprinted from a rare double issue of the French arts magazine *Verve.* Publisher's Note. 136pp. 9¼ x 12¼. 28575-8

DRAWINGS, Jean Cocteau. Portraits, scenes, literary figures, etc., all rendered with grace and wit. 129 drawings. 129pp. 8⅜ x 11¼. 20781-1

DALÍ ON MODERN ART: The Cuckolds of Antiquated Modern Art, Salvadore Dalí. Dalí's highly opinionated attack skewers both modern art and its practitioners. Outrageous evaluations of Picasso, Turner, Cézanne, and many more. Text includes 15 renderings of paintings discussed and 44 of Dalí's calligraphic decorations. 96pp. 5⅜ x 8½. (Available in U.S. only) 29220-7

50 SECRETS OF MAGIC CRAFTSMANSHIP, Salvadore Dalí. Rare, important volume in which Dalí expounds (in his inimitably eccentric fashion) on what painting should be, the history of painting, what is good and bad painting, the merits of specific artists, and more. Includes his 50 "secrets" for mastering the craft, including "the secret of the painter's pointed mustaches." Filled with sensible artistic advice, lively personal anecdotes, academic craftsmanship, and the artist's own marginal drawings. 192pp. 9¼ x 12¼. (Available in U.S. only) 27132-3

HOPPER DRAWINGS, Edward Hopper. 44 plates, reproduced directly from originals in the collection of the Whitney Museum of American Art, reveal Hopper's superb draftsmanship and evocative power. Only book devoted exclusively to Hopper's drawings. 48pp. 8¼ x 11¼. 25854-8

100 DRAWINGS, Gustav Klimt. The finest drawings of the celebrated Austrian artist–mostly nudes and seminudes taken in part from rare portfolios of 1919 and 1964–reveal the dynamics of the line in representing the human figure spontaneously and freely. Introduction. 99pp. 9⅜ x 12¼. 22446-5

KOKOSCHKA PORTRAIT AND FIGURE DRAWINGS, Oskar Kokoschka. Rich selection of 47 great drawings by modern Austro-German master: portraits, nudes, and more. His style is notable for its originality and power. 48pp. 8¼ x 11¼. (Available in U.S. only) 29297-5

THE ART NOUVEAU STYLE: A Comprehensive Guide with 264 Illustrations, Stephan Tschudi Madsen. Absorbing, exceptionally detailed study examines early trends, posters, and book illustrations, stylistic influences in architecture; furniture, jewelry, and other applied arts; plus perceptive discussions of artists associated with the movement. 488pp. 6½ x 9¼. 41794-8

MIRÓ LITHOGRAPHS, Joan Miró. 40 important lithographic prints with line and composition comparable to Miró's friend Picasso. Eerie, droll, technically brilliant and aggressive. 48pp. 8¼ x 11⅜. 24437-7

DRAWINGS OF MUCHA, Alphonse Mucha. 70 large-size illustrations trace Mucha's draftsmanship over more than 40 years: original plans and drawings for "The Seasons," Sarah Bernhardt posters, etc., all displaying marvelous technique. Introduction. 75pp. 9⅜ x 12¼. 23672-2

MUCHA'S FIGURES DÉCORATIVES, Alphonse Mucha. Figures of women, young girls, and children of both sexes in inimitable style of Art Nouveau master. His last stylebook. 40 plates in original color. 48pp. 9⅜ x 12¼. 24234-X

GRAPHIC WORKS OF EDVARD MUNCH, Edvard Munch. 90 haunting, evocative prints by first major Expressionist artist: *The Scream, Anxiety, Death Chamber, The Kiss, Madonna on the Jetty, Picking Apples, Ibsen in the Cafe of the Grand Hotel,* etc. xvii+90pp. 9 x 12. 23765-6

JOSÉ CLEMENTE OROZCO: AN AUTOBIOGRAPHY, José Clemente Orozco. Wealth of insights about great muralist's first inspirations; reflections on his life, on Mexico, on mural paintings; his relationships with other painters, and experiences in the United States. 192pp. 5⅜ x 8¼. 41819-7

OPTICAL ART: Theory and Practice, Rene Parola. First complete explanation of influential artistic movement: visual perception, psychological phenomena, principles and applications of Op Art, and more. Over 180 illustrations. 144pp. 9 x 12. 29054-9

PICASSO LINE DRAWINGS AND PRINTS, Pablo Picasso. 44 works from many periods and styles show 1905 circus family, portraits of Diaghilev, Balzac, Cubist studies, etc. 48pp. 8¼ x 11⅜. 24196-3

PICASSO LITHOGRAPHS, Pablo Picasso. 61 works over a period of 35 years. Master artist/craftsman revels in bulls, nudes, myth, artists, actors–all in the purest lithographic line. 64pp. 8¼ x 11⅜. 23949-7

THE COMPLETE GRAPHIC WORK OF JACK LEVINE, Kenneth W. Prescott and Emma Stina-Prescott. Never-before-published prints of work by major American artist/social commentator. Plate-by-plate commentaries. 84 works in all. 112pp. 9⅜ x 12¼. 24481-4

RACKHAM'S COLOR ILLUSTRATIONS FOR WAGNER'S RING, Arthur Rackham. By the time he began this work, Rackham (1867–1939) was England's leading illustrator, famous throughout the world for his fantastic interpretations of fairy tales and myths. This, his masterpiece, is regarded by some as the greatest representation of Wagner's drama ever produced. 64 illustrations. 9 vignettes. 72pp. 8⅜ x 11¼. 23779-6

RACKHAM'S FAIRY TALE ILLUSTRATIONS IN FULL COLOR, Arthur Rackham (selected and edited by Jeff Menges). Superb collection of 55 lovely plates, reproduced from rare, early editions; scenes from *Irish Fairy Tales, English Fairy Tales, Hansel and Gretel, Snowdrop and Other Tales, Little Brother & Little Sister,* and others. 64pp. 8 x 11¼. 42167-8

PHOTOGRAPHS BY MAN RAY: 105 WORKS, 1920–1934, Man Ray. Here is a treasury of Ray's finest photographic work, arranged in five groupings: general subject, female figures, women's faces, celebrity portraits, and rayographs ("cameraless" compositions, created by resting objects on unexposed film). 105 photos, including one in color. Texts by Ray and others. 128pp. 9⅜ x 12¼. 23842-3

SCHIELE DRAWINGS: 44 WORKS, Egon Schiele. Treasury of portraits, character studies, nudes, and more, by great Viennese Expressionist. Characteristic focus on inner psychological states and hidden personality traits of subjects. 48pp. 8¼ x 11⅜. 28150-7

CAMERA WORK: A PICTORIAL GUIDE, Alfred Steiglitz (edited by Marianne Fulton Margolis). The most important periodical in the history of art photography was *Camera Work,* edited and published by Alfred Stieglitz from 1903 to 1917. This volume contains all 559 illustrations that ever appeared in its pages, including hundreds of important photographs by the preeminent photographers of the time: Eduard Steichen, Alfred Stieglitz, Paul Strand, Alvin Langdon Coburn, Clarence White, and many others. 176pp. 8⅜ x 11¼. 23591-2

STEINLEN CATS, Théophile-Alexandre Steinlen. 66 drawings and 8 picture stories of great illustrator's favorite study–cats! 48pp. 8¼ x 11⅜. 23950-0

Write for free Fine Art and Art Instruction Catalog to
Dover Publications, Inc., Dept. ABI, 31 East 2nd Street, Mineola, NY 11501
Visit us online at www.doverpublications.com

Pictorial Archive

VICTORIAN HOUSEWARE, HARDWARE AND KITCHENWARE: A PICTORIAL ARCHIVE WITH OVER 2000 ILLUSTRATIONS, Ronald S. Barlow (ed.). This fascinating archive, reprinted from rare woodcut engravings and selected from hard-to-find antique trade catalogs, offers a realistic view of the furnishings of a typical 19th-century home, including andirons, ash sifters, housemaids' buckets, buttonhole cutters, sausage stuffers, seed strippers, spittoons, and hundreds of other items. Captions include size, weight, and cost. 376pp. 9⅜ x 12¼. 41727-1

BEARDSLEY'S LE MORTE DARTHUR: SELECTED ILLUSTRATIONS, Aubrey Beardsley. His illustrations for the great Thomas Malory classic made Aubrey Beardsley famous virtually overnight–and fired the imaginations of generations of artists with what became known as the "Beardsley look." This volume contains a rich selection of those splendid drawings, including floral and foliated openings, fauns and satyrs, initials, ornaments, and much more. Characters from Arthurian legend are portrayed in splendid full-page illustrations, bordered with evocative and fecund sinuosities of plant and flower. Artists and designers will find here a source of superb designs, graphics, and motifs for permission-free use. 62 black-and-white illustrations. 48pp. 8¼ x 11. 41795-6

TREASURY OF BIBLE ILLUSTRATIONS: OLD AND NEW TESTAMENTS, Julius Schnorr von Carolsfeld. All the best-loved, most-quoted Bible stories, painstakingly reproduced from a rare volume of German engravings. 179 imaginative illustrations depict 105 episodes from Old Testament, 74 scenes from New Testament–each on a separate page, with chapter, verse, King James Text. Outstanding source of permission-free art; remarkably accessible treatment of the Scriptures. x+182pp. 8⅜ x 11¼. 40703-9

3200 OLD-TIME CUTS AND ORNAMENTS, Blanche Cirker (ed.). Permission-free pictures from 1909 French typography catalog: plants, animals, religious motifs, music, carriages, boats, sports, furniture, clothing; plus borders, banners, wreaths, and other ornaments. More than 3,200 b/w illustrations. 112pp. 9⅜ x 12¼. 41732-8

A DIDEROT PICTORIAL ENCYCLOPEDIA OF TRADES AND INDUSTRY, Denis Diderot. First paperbound edition of 485 remarkable plates from the great 18th-century reference work. Permission-free plates depict vast array of arts and trades before the Industrial Revolution. Two-volume set. Total of 936pp. 9 x 12.

Vol. I: Agriculture and rural arts, fishing, art of war, metalworking, mining. Plates 1–208. 27428-4

Vol. II: Glass, masonry, carpentry, textiles, printing, leather, gold and jewelry, fashion, miscellaneous trades. Plates 209–485. Indexes of persons, places, and subjects. 27429-2

BIRDS, FLOWERS AND BUTTERFLIES STAINED GLASS PATTERN BOOK, Connie Clough Eaton. 68 exquisite full-page patterns; lush baskets, vases, garden bouquets, birds, and more. Perfectly rendered for stained glass; suitable for many other arts and crafts projects. 12 color illustrations on covers. 64pp. 8¼ x 11. 40717-9

TURN-OF-THE-CENTURY TILE DESIGNS IN FULL COLOR, L. François. 250 designs brimming with Art Nouveau flavor: beautiful floral and foliate motifs on wall tiles for bathrooms, multicolored stenciled friezes, and more. 48pp. 9¼ x 12¼. 41525-2

CHILDREN: A PICTORIAL ARCHIVE OF PERMISSION-FREE ILLUSTRATIONS, Carol Belanger Grafton (ed.). More than 850 versatile illustrations from rare sources depict engaging moppets playing with toys, dolls, and pets; riding bicycles; playing tennis and baseball; reading, sleeping; engaged in activities with other children; and in many other settings and situations. Appealing vignettes of bygone times for artists, designers, and craftworkers. 96pp. 9 x 12. 41797-2

504 DECORATIVE VIGNETTES IN FULL COLOR, Carol Belanger Grafton (ed.). Permission-free Victorian images of animals (some dressed in quaint period costumes, others fancifully displaying brief messages), angels, fans, cooks, clowns, musicians, revelers, and many others. 40467-6

OLD-TIME CHRISTMAS VIGNETTES IN FULL COLOR, Carol Belanger Grafton (ed.). 363 permission-free illustrations from vintage publications include Father Christmas, evergreen garlands, heavenly creatures, a splendidly decorated old-fashioned Christmas tree, and Victorian youngsters playing with Christmas toys, holding bouquets of holly, and much more. 40255-X

OLD-TIME NAUTICAL AND SEASHORE VIGNETTES IN FULL COLOR, Carol Belanger Grafton (ed.). More than 300 exquisite illustrations of sailors, ships, rowboats, lighthouses, swimmers, fish, shells, and other nautical motifs in a great variety of sizes, shapes, and styles–lovingly culled from rare 19th- and early-20th-century chromolithographs. 41524-4

BIG BOOK OF ANIMAL ILLUSTRATIONS, Maggie Kate (ed.). 688 up-to-date, detailed line illustrations–all permission-free–of monkeys and apes, horses, snakes, reptiles and amphibians, insects, butterflies, dinosaurs, and more, in accurate, natural poses. Index. 128pp. 9 x 12. 40464-1

422 ART NOUVEAU DESIGNS AND MOTIFS IN FULL COLOR, J. Klinger and H. Anker. Striking reproductions from a rare French portfolio of plants, animals, birds, insects, florals, abstracts, women, landscapes, and other subjects. Permission-free borders, repeating patterns, mortised cuts, corners, frames, and other configurations–all depicted in the sensuous, curvilinear Art Nouveau style. 32pp. 9¼ x 12¼. 40705-5

ANIMAL STUDIES: 550 ILLUSTRATIONS OF MAMMALS, BIRDS, FISH AND INSECTS, M. Méheut. Painstakingly reproduced from a rare original edition, this lavish bestiary features a spectacular array of creatures from the animal kingdom–mammals, fish, birds, reptiles and amphibians, and insects. Permission-free illustrations for graphics projects; marvelous browsing for antiquarians, art enthusiasts, and animal lovers. Captions. 112pp. 9⅜ x 12¼. 40266-5

THE ART NOUVEAU STYLE BOOK OF ALPHONSE MUCHA, Alphonse Mucha. Fine permission-free reproductions of all plates in Mucha's innovative portfolio, including designs for jewelry, wallpaper, stained glass, furniture, and tableware, plus figure studies, plant and animal motifs, and more. 18 plates in full color, 54 in 2 or more colors. Only complete one-volume edition. 80pp. 9⅜ x 12¼. 24044-4

ELEGANT FLORAL DESIGNS FOR ARTISTS AND CRAFTSPEOPLE, Marty Noble. More than 150 exquisite designs depict borders of fanciful flowers; filigreed compositions of floral sprays, wreaths, and single blossoms; delicate butterflies with wings displaying a patchwork mosaic; nosegays wrapped in lacy horns; and much more. A graceful, permission-free garden of flowers for use by illustrators, commercial artists, designers, and craftworkers. 64pp. 8⅜ x 11. 42177-5

SNOWFLAKE DESIGNS, Marty Noble and Eric Gottesman. More than 120 intricate, permission-free images of snowflakes, based on actual photographs, are ideal for use in textile and wallpaper designs, needlework and craft projects, and other creative applications. iv+44pp. 8¼ x 11. 41526-0

ART NOUVEAU FIGURATIVE DESIGNS, Ed Sibbett, Jr. Art Nouveau goddesses, nymphs, florals from posters, decorations by Alphonse Mucha. 3 gorgeous designs. 48pp. 8¼ x 11. 23444-4

ANTIQUE FURNITURE AND DECORATIVE ACCESSORIES: A PICTORIAL ARCHIVE WITH 3,500 ILLUSTRATIONS, Thomas Arthur Strange. Cathedral stalls, altar pieces, sofas, commodes, writing tables, grillwork, organs, pulpits, and other decorative accessories produced by such noted craftsmen as Inigo Jones, Christopher Wren, Sheraton, Hepplewhite, and Chippendale. Descriptive text. 376pp. 8⅜ x 11¼. 41224-5

ART NOUVEAU FLORAL PATTERNS AND STENCIL DESIGNS IN FULL COLOR, M. P. Verneuil. Permission-free art from two rare turn-of-the-century portfolios *(Etude de la Plante* and *L'ornementation par le Pochoir)* includes 159 floral and foliate motifs by M. P. Verneuil, one of the Art Nouveau movement's finest artists. The collection includes 120 images of flowers–foxglove, hollyhocks, columbine, lilies, and others–and 39 stencil designs of blossoming trees, reeds, mushrooms, oak leaves, peacocks, and more. 80pp. 9¼ x 12¼. 40126-X

*Write for **free** Fine Art and Art Instruction Catalog to*
Dover Publications, Inc., Dept. ABI, 31 East 2nd Street, Mineola, NY 11501
*Visit us online at **www.doverpublications.com***